Trevor Senior

# ESSENTIALS
## Edexcel
## GCSE Maths
### Higher Tier
### Revision Guide

# Contents

|  |  | Maths B<br>Unit Reference | Revised |
|---|---|---|---|

# Contents

# Rounding

## Rounding and Approximation

Numbers are **rounded**:

- to **estimate** the answer to a calculation using **approximate** values
- to give a sensible answer.

## Estimating Values of Calculations

When you approximate the value of a number always work to 1 **significant figure** (see page 5). For example, 18.8 approximates to 20 using 1 significant figure.

> **Example 1**
>
> Use approximations to estimate the answer to:
>
> $$\frac{5020}{4.9 \times 20.8}$$
>
> **Solution**
>
> 5020 = 5000 to 1 significant figure
>
> 4.9 = 5 to 1 significant figure
>
> 20.8 = 20 to 1 significant figure
>
> $$\frac{5000}{5 \times 20} = 50$$

> **Example 2**
>
> Use approximations to estimate the value of:
>
> $$\frac{19.7 \times 30.1}{0.59}$$
>
> **Solution**
>
> Rounding each number to 1 significant figure
>
> $$\frac{19.7 \times 30.1}{0.59} \text{ is approximately } \frac{20 \times 30}{0.6}$$
>
> $$\frac{20 \times 30}{0.6} = \frac{600}{0.6}$$
>
> To remove the decimal from this calculation, multiply the numerator and denominator by 10
>
> $$= \frac{6000}{6} = 1000$$
>
> So $\frac{19.7 \times 30.1}{0.59}$ is approximately 1000

# Rounding

## Decimal Places

Look at the number **27.35083**

To round to 1 **decimal place**, look at the **second** decimal place:

- If the second decimal place has a value of 5 or more, round up the number in the first decimal place.
- If the second decimal place has a value of less than 5, leave the number in the first decimal place unchanged.

To round to **2 decimal places**, look at the **third** decimal place, and so on.

So:

- 27.3│5083 = 27.4 to 1 decimal place (i.e. 3 rounds up to 4)
- 27.35│083 = 27.35 to 2 decimal places (i.e. 5 stays unchanged)
- 27.350│83 = 27.351 to 3 decimal places (i.e. 0 rounds up to 1).

## Significant Figures

The first **significant figure** is the first non-zero digit from the left.

Look again at the number **27.35083**

To round to 1 significant figure, look at the **second** significant figure:

- If the second significant figure has a value of 5 or more, round up the first significant figure.
- If the second significant figure has a value of less than 5, leave the first significant figure unchanged.

To round to **2 significant figures**, look at the **third** significant figure, and so on.

Use zeros to keep the place value of the significant figures.

So:

- 2│7.35083 = 30 to 1 significant figure (i.e. 2 rounds up to 3 and put a zero in the units column)
- 27.│35083 = 27 to 2 significant figures (i.e. 7 stays unchanged)
- 27.3│5083 = 27.4 to 3 significant figures (i.e. 3 rounds up to 4).

### Example

Write the number 0.03053 to 2 significant figures.

**Solution**
The first significant figure is the digit 3.

So 0.030│53 = 0.031 to 2 significant figures.

*0 is followed by a 5, so round up to 1*

*The leading zeros are used to keep the place value of the significant figures*

## Quick Test

1. Round the following numbers to:
   - i) 1 decimal place
   - ii) 2 decimal places
   - iii) 1 significant figure
   - iv) 2 significant figures.
   - a) 18.725  b) 0.0725  c) 2436.518

2. Use approximations to estimate the value of each of the following:
   - a) $\dfrac{71.2 + 28.8}{9.5}$  b) $\dfrac{4.15 \times 38.7}{7.69}$
   - c) $\dfrac{99.9 \times 5.87}{0.29}$

# Multiples and Factors

## Order of Operations

**BIDMAS** is a way of remembering the order to carry out operations. Simplify **brackets** first, then work out any **indices** (powers) and finally **divide**, **multiply**, **add** and **subtract** in that order:

- **B**rackets, e.g. $2 \times (8 + 3) = 2 \times 11 = 22$
- **I**ndices (or powers), e.g. $3^2 \times (7 - 2)^2 = 3^2 \times 5^2$
  $= 9 \times 25 = 225$
- **D**ivision, e.g. $3 + 4^2 \div 2 = 3 + 16 \div 2 = 3 + 8 = 11$
- **M**ultiplication, e.g. $3 \times 8 \div 2 + 1$
  $= 3 \times 4 + 1 = 12 + 1 = 13$
- **A**ddition, e.g. $3 + 5 \times 4^2 = 3 + 5 \times 16$
  $= 3 + 80 = 83$
- **S**ubtraction, e.g. $3 \times 10 \div 2 - 1 + 4$
  $= 3 \times 5 - 1 + 4 = 15 - 1 + 4 = 18$

## Number Facts

You should know these sets of numbers:
- **Even numbers**: 2, 4, 6, 8, 10…
- **Odd numbers**: 1, 3, 5, 7, 9…
- **Prime numbers**: 2, 3, 5, 7, 11…

**Multiples** of a number are found by multiplying the number by another **integer**. For example:
- multiples of 3 are 3, 6, 9, 12, 15…
- multiples of 7 are 7, 14, 21, 28, 35…

**Factors** of a number are all the whole numbers that divide into it exactly. For example:
- factors of 17 are 1 and 17
- factors of 18 are 1, 2, 3, 6, 9 and 18
- factors of 25 are 1, 5 and 25.

*N.B. Prime numbers only have two factors – the number itself and 1.*

## Product of Prime Factors

**Prime factors** are factors of a number that are also prime.

### Example

Write 24 as a **product** of prime factors.

**Solution A**
Using a factor tree:

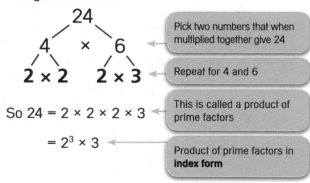

Pick two numbers that when multiplied together give 24

Repeat for 4 and 6

So $24 = 2 \times 2 \times 2 \times 3$

This is called a product of prime factors

$= 2^3 \times 3$

Product of prime factors in **index form**

**Solution B**
Using prime factor decomposition:

$$\begin{array}{c|c} 2 & 24 \\ 2 & 12 \\ 2 & 6 \\ 3 & 3 \\ & 1 \end{array}$$

2 is prime and is a factor of 24, so $24 \div 2 = 12$

2 is also a factor of 12, so $12 \div 2 = 6$

2 is also a factor of 6, so $6 \div 2 = 3$

3 is prime and is a factor of itself, so $3 \div 3 = 1$

So $24 = 2 \times 2 \times 2 \times 3$

$= 2^3 \times 3$

**Key Words**   BIDMAS • Even number • Odd number • Prime number • Multiple • Integer • Factor

# Multiples and Factors

## Least Common Multiple and Highest Common Factor

### Least Common Multiple (LCM)

The **least common multiple** (or lowest common multiple) of two numbers is the lowest number that is in the multiplication tables of both numbers.

#### Example 1

Work out the least common multiple of 5 and 8.

**Solution**

Multiples of 5 are:
5, 10, 15, 20, 25, 30, 35, (40), 45…

Multiples of 8 are:
8, 16, 24, 32, (40), 48, 56…

40 is the lowest number in both lists, so 40 is the least common multiple.

#### Example 2

Work out the highest common factor of 24 and 40.

**Solution**

The factors of 24 are:
1, 2, 3, 4, 6, (8), 12 and 24.

The factors of 40 are:
1, 2, 4, 5, (8), 10, 20 and 40.

8 is the highest number in both lists, so 8 is the highest common factor.

### Highest Common Factor (HCF)

The **highest common factor** of two numbers is the highest number that divides into both numbers.

#### Example 3

The least common multiple of two numbers is 24. The highest common factor of the same two numbers is 4.

Work out the two numbers.

**Solution**

> **Problem Solving**
>
> Break this type of question into several steps. Start by listing the multiples of 4 as you know that 4 is a factor of both numbers.

Multiples of 4 are 4, 8, 12, 16, 20, 24…

Numbers in this list which are factors of 24 are 8, 12 and 24.

The two numbers must be 8 and 12 to satisfy both conditions.

## Quick Test

1. Work out the following:
   a) $(6 - 4) \times (5 + 2)$    b) $5^3 + 50 \div 10$    c) $3^2 + 4^2 + 5^2 \times 2$
2. Write 60 as a product of prime factors. Give your answer in index form.
3. Work out the least common multiple of the following:
   a) 8 and 10    b) 4 and 7    c) 6 and 9
4. Work out the highest common factor of the following:
   a) 20 and 28    b) 15 and 25    c) 12 and 30

# Fractions

## Equivalent Fractions

**Equivalent fractions** are fractions that can be simplified (cancelled down) to the same value.

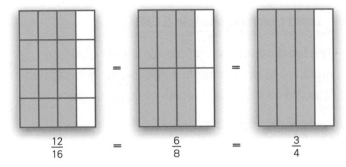

$$\frac{12}{16} = \frac{6}{8} = \frac{3}{4}$$

## Adding and Subtracting Fractions

To add or subtract fractions they must have the same **denominator**.

### Example 1

Work out $2\frac{2}{3} + 1\frac{1}{2}$

**Solution**

$2\frac{2}{3} + 1\frac{1}{2} = 2 + 1 + \frac{2}{3} + \frac{1}{2}$

$= 3 + \frac{4}{6} + \frac{3}{6}$ ← $= 3 + \frac{7}{6}$

$= 3 + 1\frac{1}{6}$

$= 4\frac{1}{6}$

### Example 2

Work out $4\frac{1}{4} - 2\frac{1}{2}$

**Solution A**

$4\frac{1}{4} - 2\frac{1}{2} = 4 - 2 + \frac{1}{4} - \frac{1}{2}$

$= 2 - \frac{1}{4} = 1\frac{3}{4}$

**Solution B**

$4\frac{1}{4} - 2\frac{1}{2} = \frac{17}{4} - \frac{5}{2}$ ← Here we are changing the mixed numbers to improper fractions

$= \frac{17}{4} - \frac{10}{4}$

$= \frac{7}{4}$

$= 1\frac{3}{4}$

## Multiplying Fractions

To multiply fractions:

1. change any **mixed numbers** to **improper fractions**
2. multiply the **numerators** together
3. multiply the denominators together
4. simplify the answer if possible.

### Example 1

Work out $\frac{3}{4} \times \frac{3}{5}$

**Solution**

$\frac{3}{4} \times \frac{3}{5} = \frac{9}{20}$

### Example 2

Work out $2\frac{2}{3} \times 1\frac{1}{5}$

**Solution**

$2\frac{2}{3} \times 1\frac{1}{5} = \frac{8}{3} \times \frac{6}{5}$

$= \frac{8}{3^1} \times \frac{6^2}{5}$ ← Simplify by cancelling by 3

$= \frac{16}{5}$

$= 3\frac{1}{5}$

**Key Words** Equivalent fraction • Denominator • Mixed number • Improper fraction • Numerator

## Dividing Fractions

To divide fractions:

**1** change any mixed numbers to improper fractions

**2** turn the second fraction upside down and change the division to multiplication

**3** do the multiplication as shown on page 8.

**Example 1**

Work out $\frac{5}{6} \div \frac{3}{5}$

**Solution**

$\frac{5}{6} \div \frac{3}{5} = \frac{5}{6} \times \frac{5}{3}$

$\phantom{\frac{5}{6} \div \frac{3}{5}} = \frac{25}{18}$

$\phantom{\frac{5}{6} \div \frac{3}{5}} = 1\frac{7}{18}$

**Example 2**

Work out $1\frac{1}{4} \div 2\frac{1}{3}$

**Solution**

$1\frac{1}{4} \div 2\frac{1}{3} = \frac{5}{4} \div \frac{7}{3}$

$\phantom{1\frac{1}{4} \div 2\frac{1}{3}} = \frac{5}{4} \times \frac{3}{7}$

$\phantom{1\frac{1}{4} \div 2\frac{1}{3}} = \frac{15}{28}$

## Fractions of Quantities

To calculate a fraction of a quantity, multiply the fraction by the quantity.

To write a quantity as a fraction of another quantity:

**1** match the units

**2** write the fraction and simplify.

**Example 1**

$\frac{3}{4}$ of the 28 students in a class are boys. How many are girls?

**Solution**

| Problem Solving |
| --- |
| You can either work out $\frac{1}{4}$ of 28 for the number of girls or $\frac{3}{4}$ of 28 for the number of boys and then subtract this from the total number of students. |

$\frac{3}{4}$ of 28 $= \frac{3}{4} \times 28$

$\phantom{\frac{3}{4} \text{ of } 28} = \frac{3}{\cancel{4}^1} \times \frac{\cancel{28}^7}{1} = 21$

There are 21 boys, so there are:

$28 - 21 = 7$ girls

**Example 2**

Write 30 cm as a fraction of 1 metre.

**Solution**

1 metre = 100 cm ← Make the units the same

So 30 cm as a fraction of 1 metre is $\frac{30\ cm}{100\ cm} = \frac{3}{10}$

**Example 3**

In two tests, Nicholas gets 13 out of 15 and 16 out of 20.

Which is the better score?

**Solution**

| Problem Solving |
| --- |
| To compare the two scores, one way is to write them as fractions with common denominators. Then compare the numerators. |

13 out of 15 is $\frac{13}{15} = \frac{52}{60}$ ← Multiply the numerator and denominator by 4

16 out of 20 is $\frac{16}{20} = \frac{48}{60}$ ← Multiply the numerator and denominator by 3

So 13 out of 15 is the better score.

## Quick Test

**1** Work out the following:

    **a)** $1\frac{1}{4} + 3\frac{1}{3}$    **b)** $2\frac{3}{5} - 1\frac{1}{4}$    **c)** $1\frac{1}{2} \times 1\frac{1}{3}$    **d)** $3\frac{4}{5} \div 2\frac{1}{6}$

**2** Work out $\frac{2}{3}$ of £60.

**3** Write 50 grams as a fraction of 1 kilogram. *(Hint: 1 kg = 1000 g)*

# Percentages

## Calculating a Percentage of a Quantity

To calculate a **percentage** of a **quantity**:
1. change the percentage to a fraction or a decimal fraction
2. calculate the fraction of the quantity.

**Example**

Work out 80% of 200 grams.

**Solution**

80% of 200 grams is $\frac{80}{100} \times 200 = 160$ grams

## One Quantity as a Percentage of Another Quantity

To express one quantity as a percentage of another quantity:
1. make sure both quantities are in the same units
2. express the quantity as a fraction of the other quantity
3. change the fraction to a percentage.

**Example**

Express 50p as a percentage of £2.

**Solution**

50p as a percentage of 200p $= \frac{50}{200} \times 100 = 25\%$

## Increasing or Decreasing Quantities by a Percentage

To increase or decrease a quantity by a percentage:
- work out the increase and add it on
- work out the decrease and subtract it.

Alternatively:
- write down the **multiplier**
- multiply the original amount by the multiplier.

**Example 1**

Jo's pay is £17 000 per year. She gets a 5% pay rise. Work out her new pay.

**Solution A**

5% of £17 000

$= \frac{5}{100} \times 17\,000$

$= £850$

New pay is 17 000 + 850 = £17 850

**Solution B (Multiplier method)**

5% extra is the same as 100% + 5% = 105%

$105\% = \frac{105}{100} = 1.05$ ← The decimal equivalent is called the **multiplier**

105% of £17 000

$= 1.05 \times 17\,000$

$= £17\,850$

**Example 2**

Which offer is better value?

Offer 1          Offer 2

**Solution**

| Problem Solving |
| --- |
| When asked which is the 'better value' always work out the cost for the same quantity so that you can compare. |

Offer 1 = 1000 g for £2.25

Offer 2 = 750 g for £1.80

Offer 1 would cost $\frac{£2.25}{4} = 56.25$p

Offer 2 would cost $\frac{£1.80}{3} = 60$p

Work out the cost of 250 g

So Offer 1 is better value.

## Percentage Change

To work out **percentage change**:

**1** work out the change, e.g. increase, decrease, profit or loss

**2** use the formula shown.

$$\text{Percentage change} = \frac{\text{change}}{\text{original amount}} \times 100\%$$

**Example**

Mr Smith bought a ring for £250 and sold it for £400. Work out his percentage profit.

**Solution**

$$\text{Percentage profit} = \frac{\text{profit}}{\text{original amount}} \times 100\%$$

$$= \frac{150}{250} \times 100 \quad \longleftarrow \quad \boxed{\text{Profit is £400} - \text{£250} = \text{£150}}$$

$$= 60\%$$

## Compound and Reverse Percentages

### Compound Percentages

A **compound percentage** is a repeated percentage calculation.

**Example**

£2000 is invested at 5% per annum compound interest. Work out the value after 2 years.

**Solution A**

5% of £2000 is £100 $\longleftarrow$ So after 1 year the investment is worth £2100

5% of £2100 is £105

So after 2 years the investment is worth £2205.

**Solution B (Multiplier method)**

5% gives a multiplier of 1.05

So after 2 years the investment is worth:

$$2000 \times 1.05 \times 1.05 = £2205$$

### Reverse Percentages

**Reverse percentage** involves working backwards from the **final amount** to the **original amount**.

**Example**

Work out the original price of the TV.

20% OFF
SALE PRICE: £496

**Solution**

20% off means it is 100% − 20% = 80% of the original price.

So 80% is £496

$$1\% \text{ is } \frac{496}{80}$$

Original price (100%) is:

$$\frac{496}{80} \times 100 = £620$$

## Quick Test

**1** Work out 30% of 600 grams.

**2** Express 25 cm as a percentage of 3 metres.

**3 a)** Increase £14 by 20%  **b)** Decrease 120 minutes by 35%

**4** Work out the value of £1000 invested for 3 years at 4% compound interest.

**5** The number of workers in an office was reduced to 12. This is a 20% reduction. How many used to work in the office?

# Powers and Roots

## Square and Cube Numbers

You need to know all the **square numbers** up to $15^2 = 225$

| $1^2 =$ | $2^2 =$ | $3^2 =$ | $4^2 =$ | $5^2 =$ | $6^2 =$ | $7^2 =$ | $8^2 =$ |
|---|---|---|---|---|---|---|---|
| 1 | 4 | 9 | 16 | 25 | 36 | 49 | 64 |

| $9^2 =$ | $10^2 =$ | $11^2 =$ | $12^2 =$ | $13^2 =$ | $14^2 =$ | $15^2 =$ |
|---|---|---|---|---|---|---|
| 81 | 100 | 121 | 144 | 169 | 196 | 225 |

You need to know the following **cube numbers**:

| $1^3 =$ | $2^3 =$ | $3^3 =$ | $4^3 =$ | $5^3 =$ | $10^3 =$ |
|---|---|---|---|---|---|
| 1 | 8 | 27 | 64 | 125 | 1000 |

You also need to know the corresponding **square roots** and **cube roots**, e.g. $\sqrt{121} = 11$ and $\sqrt[3]{64} = 4$

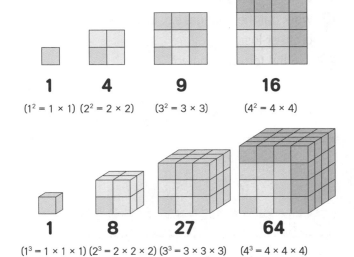

1     4     9     16

$(1^2 = 1 \times 1)$   $(2^2 = 2 \times 2)$   $(3^2 = 3 \times 3)$   $(4^2 = 4 \times 4)$

1     8     27     64

$(1^3 = 1 \times 1 \times 1)$ $(2^3 = 2 \times 2 \times 2)$ $(3^3 = 3 \times 3 \times 3)$   $(4^3 = 4 \times 4 \times 4)$

## Working with Powers and Roots

The **power** or **index** (plural: indices) of a number is the number of times a number is multiplied by itself, e.g. $5^3 = 5 \times 5 \times 5$ and $2^4 = 2 \times 2 \times 2 \times 2$

When working with indices, follow these rules:
- To multiply powers of the same number, add the indices.
  $3^4 \times 3^5 = 3^{(4 + 5)} = 3^9$
- To divide powers of the same number, subtract the indices.
  $6^7 \div 6^2 = 6^{(7 - 2)} = 6^5$
- To work out the power of a number to another power, multiply the indices.
  $(10^2)^3 = 10^6$ (1 million)
- Any number to the power 1 is itself.
  $8^1 = 8$
- Any number to the power zero is 1.
  $4^0 = 1$
- Any number to a **negative power** is the **reciprocal** of the same number to the positive power.
  $9^{-2} = \frac{1}{9^2} = \frac{1}{81}$

Make sure that you know how to work with powers and roots on your calculator.

For example:

| Input | Keys | Display |
|---|---|---|
| $24^2$ | ( 2 ) ( 4 ) ( $x^2$ ) ( = ) | 576 |
| $\sqrt{289}$ | ( $\sqrt{\blacksquare}$ ) ( 2 ) ( 8 ) ( 9 ) ( = ) | 17 |
| $10^6$ | ( 1 ) ( 0 ) ( $x^{\blacksquare}$ ) ( 6 ) ( = ) | 1 000 000 |
| $5^{-1}$ | ( 5 ) ( $x^{-1}$ ) ( = ) | 0.2 |
| $\sqrt[3]{90}$ | ( SHIFT ) ( $\sqrt[3]{\blacksquare}$ ) ( 9 ) ( 0 ) ( = ) | 4.481... |

Your calculator may work differently to the examples above. Make sure you know how it works.

Rules of indices also work in algebra. For example:
- $x^4 \times x^5 = x^{(4 + 5)} = x^9$
- $x^7 \div x^2 = x^{(7 - 2)} = x^5$
- $(x^2)^3 = x^6$

    Square number • Cube number • Square root • Cube root • Power • Index

## Example 1

a) Simplify $\dfrac{4^6 \times 4^2}{4^5}$

**Solution**

$\dfrac{4^6 \times 4^2}{4^5} = \dfrac{4^8}{4^5} = 4^3$

b) Work out the value of $\dfrac{3^2 \times 3^3}{3^7}$

**Solution**

$\dfrac{3^2 \times 3^3}{3^7} = \dfrac{3^5}{3^7}$

$= 3^{-2}$

$= \dfrac{1}{3^2}$

$= \dfrac{1}{9}$

## Example 2

Which is greater, $5^0$ or $5^{-2}$?

**Solution**

**Problem Solving**

Use the rules of indices to work out the values and remember to say which is greater.

$5^0 = 1$

$5^{-2} = \dfrac{1}{5^2} = \dfrac{1}{25}$

1 is greater than $\frac{1}{25}$, so $5^0$ is greater than $5^{-2}$.

## Fractional Powers (Roots)

A **fractional power** is a root:
- Power $\frac{1}{2}$ is the positive square root.
- Power $\frac{1}{3}$ is the cube root, and so on.

## Example 1

Work out the value of:

a) $25^{\frac{1}{2}}$

**Solution**

$25^{\frac{1}{2}} = \sqrt{25} = 5$

b) $16^{\frac{1}{4}}$

**Solution**

$16^{\frac{1}{4}} = \sqrt[4]{16} = 2$

Because $2 \times 2 \times 2 \times 2 = 16$

c) $8^{\frac{2}{3}}$

**Solution**

$8^{\frac{2}{3}} = \left(\sqrt[3]{8}\right)^2 = 2^2 = 4$

It's always easier to work out the root first

## Example 2

Work out the value of:

a) $16^{-\frac{1}{4}}$

**Solution**

$16^{-\frac{1}{4}} = \dfrac{1}{16^{\frac{1}{4}}} = \dfrac{1}{\sqrt[4]{16}} = \dfrac{1}{2}$

b) $125^{-\frac{2}{3}}$

**Solution**

$125^{-\frac{2}{3}} = \dfrac{1}{125^{\frac{2}{3}}} = \dfrac{1}{\left(\sqrt[3]{125}\right)^2} = \dfrac{1}{5^2} = \dfrac{1}{25}$

## Quick Test

1 Write down the value of:
a) $12^2$ 149  b) $3^3$ 27
c) $\sqrt{169}$ 13  d) $\sqrt[3]{1000}$ 10

2 Work out the values of:
a) $36^{\frac{1}{2}}$ 6  b) $125^{\frac{1}{3}}$ 5
c) $8^{-\frac{1}{3}}$  d) $27^{-\frac{2}{3}}$ 1/9

# Standard Index Form

## Standard Form

**Standard form** or **standard index form** is a way of writing numbers using **powers of 10**. The number to be expressed in standard form is written as a number between 1 and 10 and multiplied by a power of 10:

$a \times 10^n$ where $1 \leqslant a < 10$ and $n$ is a whole number

Remember these points about $n$:

- For **large** numbers $n$ is **positive**.
- For **small** numbers (fractions less than 1) $n$ is **negative**.
- The value of $n$ tells you how many **places** the digits have moved.

### Example 1

Write in standard form:

**a)** 24.3

**Solution**
$24.3 = 2.43 \times 10^1$ ← Digits have moved one place to the right

**b)** 6471

**Solution**
$6471 = 6.471 \times 10^3$ ← Digits have moved three places to the right

**c)** 500

**Solution**
$500 = 5 \times 10^2$ ← Digits have moved two places to the right

**d)** 0.048

**Solution**
$0.048 = 4.8 \times 10^{-2}$ ← Digits have moved two places to the left

**e)** 0.002

**Solution**
$0.002 = 2 \times 10^{-3}$ ← Digits have moved three places to the left

**f)** 9.61

**Solution**
$9.61 = 9.61 \times 10^0$ ← Digits haven't moved

### Example 2

Write these numbers in order starting with the smallest:

$$1.6 \times 10^5 \qquad 2.5 \times 10^4 \qquad 2.1 \times 10^5$$

**Solution**

**Problem Solving**

When asked to order numbers in standard form, sort them by order of powers first – the higher the power, the bigger the value.

The middle number is the smallest as it has the lowest power.

The others have the same power but 1.6 is smaller than 2.1

So in order the numbers are:
$$2.5 \times 10^4 \qquad 1.6 \times 10^5 \qquad 2.1 \times 10^5$$

## Calculations with Standard Form

Numbers in standard form can be keyed into a calculator. To enter the number $1.2 \times 10^7$ key in as shown.

The calculator will display the numbers either as an **ordinary number** or in standard form.

Or:

## Adding or Subtracting Numbers Given in Standard Form

To add or subtract numbers given in standard form, write
them as ordinary numbers and then do the calculation.

**Example**

Work out:

**a)** $2.5 \times 10^3 + 8.9 \times 10^4$

**Solution**
$2.5 \times 10^3 + 8.9 \times 10^4 = 2500 + 89\,000$

$= 91\,500$ or $9.15 \times 10^4$

**b)** $2.3 \times 10^{-1} - 7.7 \times 10^{-2}$

**Solution**
$2.3 \times 10^{-1} - 7.7 \times 10^{-2} = 0.23 - 0.077$

$= 0.153$ or $1.53 \times 10^{-1}$

## Multiplying or Dividing Numbers Given in Standard Form

To multiply or divide numbers given in standard form,
work out the numbers and the powers separately.
Check that the answer is in standard form.

**Example**

Work out:

**a)** $2.1 \times 10^3 \times 4 \times 10^4$

**Solution**
$2.1 \times 10^3 \times 4 \times 10^4$

$= (2.1 \times 4) \times (10^3 \times 10^4)$

$= 8.4 \times 10^7$ ← Add the powers of 10

**b)** $6.9 \times 10^3 \div 1.5 \times 10^{-3}$

**Solution**
$6.9 \times 10^3 \div 1.5 \times 10^{-3}$

$= (6.9 \div 1.5) \times (10^3 \div 10^{-3})$

$= 4.6 \times 10^6$ ← Subtract the powers of 10

**c)** $4.2 \times 10^3 \times 9.4 \times 10^2$

**Solution**
$4.2 \times 10^3 \times 9.4 \times 10^2$

$= (4.2 \times 9.4) \times (10^3 \times 10^2)$

$= 39.48 \times 10^5$ ← Note that this isn't in standard form

$= 3.948 \times 10^1 \times 10^5$

$= 3.948 \times 10^6$

## Quick Test

1. Write these numbers in standard form:
   **a)** 372 **b)** 6000 **c)** 0.023 **d)** 5.67

2. Write these as ordinary numbers:
   **a)** $3.14 \times 10^2$ **b)** $2.1 \times 10^4$ **c)** $3.65 \times 10^{-1}$ **d)** $5.8 \times 10^{-2}$

3. Work out:
   **a)** $3.6 \times 10^2 + 1.7 \times 10^3$ **b)** $8.1 \times 10^2 - 2.4 \times 10^3$ **c)** $3.9 \times 10^2 \times 6.2 \times 10^3$ **d)** $\dfrac{4 \times 10^6}{8 \times 10^9}$

# Ratio

## Simplifying a Ratio

A **ratio** (:) is used to compare two or more quantities.

> **Example 1**
>
> Express 30 cm to 2 metres as a ratio in its simplest form.
>
> **Solution**
>
> 30 cm : 2 metres = 30 cm : 200 cm ← When working with ratios, always use common units so they can cancel out
>
> = 3 : 20

> **Example 2**
>
> The scale on a map is given as 1 cm to 2 km. Express this as a ratio in its simplest form.
>
> **Solution**
>
> 1 km = 1000 metres; 1 metre = 100 cm
>
> So 2 km = 200 000 cm ← Change to a common unit
>
> The ratio of the map is 1 cm : 200 000 cm
>
> = 1 : 200 000 ← Cancel out the units

## Ratios as Fractions

A ratio can be written as a fraction.

> **Example**
>
> Matthew and Natasha share a pizza in the ratio 3 : 2
>
> What fraction does Matthew eat?
>
> **Solution**
>
> | **Problem Solving** |
> | --- |
> | Use the total number of parts in the ratio to represent the total number of pieces of pizza. Then write the number Matthew eats as a fraction of the total number of pieces. |
>
> The ratio has 5 parts altogether.
>
> Matthew eats 3 out of the 5 pieces, so he eats $\frac{3}{5}$ of the pizza.

## Dividing a Quantity in a Given Ratio

You can share quantities by using ratio. The parts in the ratio represent the proportions.

### Example 1

An orange drink is made of orange juice and water in the ratio 1 : 4

How much water is used in a 200 ml drink?

**Solution**

There are 4 + 1 = 5 parts in the ratio altogether. So 5 parts is 200 ml.

1 part is 40 ml ⟵ *Dividing by 5*

4 parts are 160 ml ⟵ *Multiplying by 4*

So 160 ml of water is used.

### Example 2

The ratio of adults to children at a football match is 7 : 3. There are 1500 children at the match. How many more adults are there than children?

> **Problem Solving**
> Always start by working out one part. Then work out how many more parts are for adults than children or work out the number of adults.

**Solution A**

Children represent 3 parts of the ratio.

So 3 parts = 1500

1 part = 500 ⟵ *Dividing by 3*

Adults represent 4 more parts than children in the ratio.

So 4 parts = 2000 ⟵ *Multiplying by 4*

There are 2000 more adults than children.

**Solution B**

Children represent 3 parts of the ratio.

So 3 parts = 1500

1 part = 500 ⟵ *Dividing by 3*

Adults represent 7 parts.

So 7 parts = 3500 ⟵ *500 × 7*

3500 − 1500 = 2000 more adults than children

## Quick Test

1. Write these ratios as simply as possible:
   a) 5 : 35     b) 66 : 44     c) 5 cm : 1 m     d) 2 kg : 400 g
2. $\frac{1}{3}$ of the students in a class are girls.
   a) Write the number of girls to the number of boys as a ratio.
   b) There are 18 boys. How many girls are there?
3. Divide £36 in the ratio 4 : 5
4. Work out the largest part if 180 kg is divided in the ratio 2 : 3 : 5

# Proportion

## Direct Proportion

Two values are in **direct proportion** if the ratio between them remains fixed as the values change.

> **Example**
>
> If 2 bags of flour cost £2.36, how much do 3 cost?
>
> **Solution**
>
> 1 bag costs $\frac{2.36}{2}$ = £1.18
>
> So 3 bags cost 1.18 × 3 = £3.54

## Speed, Distance and Time

To measure **speed** you need to know the **distance** travelled and the **time** taken.

$$\text{Speed} = \frac{\text{distance}}{\text{time}}$$

The **units** for speed are usually one of:
- miles per hour (mph)
- kilometres per hour (km/h)
- metres per second (m/s).

At constant speed, distance is **directly proportional** to time.

> **Example**
>
> A car travels 150 metres in 10 seconds. How far will it travel in 30 seconds at the same speed?
>
> **Solution**
>
> The car will travel
> 15 metres in 1 second.    ← Speed = 15 m/s
>
> It will travel 15 × 30
> = 450 metres in 30 seconds    ← Distance = speed × time

## Density

To measure the **density** of an object you need to know the **mass** and the **volume**.

$$\text{Density} = \frac{\text{mass}}{\text{volume}}$$

The units for density are usually one of:
- grams per centimetre cubed (g/cm³)
- kilograms per metre cubed (kg/m³)

At a constant density, mass is **directly proportional** to volume.

> **Example**
>
> An object has mass 120 grams and volume 30 cm³. Work out the mass of a similar object that has a volume 8 times as big.
>
> **Solution A**
>
> As the volume is 8 times as big, the mass will be 8 times more. So mass is 120 × 8
> = 960 grams
>
> **Solution B**
>
> Density is $\frac{120}{30}$ = 4 g/cm³    ← Density = $\frac{\text{mass}}{\text{volume}}$
>
> So for the similar object the volume is:
> 30 × 8 = 240 cm³
>
> So the mass of the similar object is:
> 240 × 4 = 960 grams    ← Mass = volume × density

## Direct Proportion Graphs

If two quantities $y$ and $x$ are **directly proportional**, we write $y \alpha x$ or $y = kx$ where k is called the **constant of proportionality**. The graph will be a straight line through the origin.

This is the graph $y = 2x$ so every $y$-value is twice the corresponding $x$-value.

$y$ can also be directly proportional to $x^2$ ($y \alpha x^2$), $x^3$ ($y \alpha x^3$), $\sqrt{x}$ ($y \alpha \sqrt{x}$), $\sqrt[3]{x}$ ($y \alpha \sqrt[3]{x}$), and so on.

**Example**

$y$ is directly proportional to the square of $x$.
When $y = 18$, $x = 3$

Work out the value of $y$ when $x = 5$

**Solution**
We write $y \alpha x^2$ or $y = kx^2$

$y = 18$, $x = 3$, so $18 = k \times 3^2$, giving k = 2

So $y = 2x^2$

When $x = 5$, $y = 2 \times 5^2 = 50$

## Indirect (Inverse) Proportion Graphs

Two values are **indirectly** (or **inversely**) **proportional** if as one value increases, the other decreases in the same ratio, e.g. as one doubles, the other halves.

If two quantities $y$ and $x$ are indirectly proportional, we write $y \alpha \frac{1}{x}$ or $y = \frac{k}{x}$

The graph will be a **reciprocal** curve as shown.

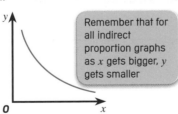

Remember that for all indirect proportion graphs as $x$ gets bigger, $y$ gets smaller

$y$ can also be indirectly proportional to $x^2$ $\left(y \alpha \frac{1}{x^2}\right)$, $x^3$ $\left(y \alpha \frac{1}{x^3}\right)$, $\sqrt{x}$ $\left(y \alpha \frac{1}{\sqrt{x}}\right)$, $\sqrt[3]{x}$ $\left(y \alpha \frac{1}{\sqrt[3]{x}}\right)$, and so on.

**Example**

$y$ is indirectly proportional to the cube root of $x$.
When $y = 2$, $x = 8$

Work out the value of $y$ when $x = 27$

**Solution**
We write $y \alpha \frac{1}{\sqrt[3]{x}}$ or $y = \frac{k}{\sqrt[3]{x}}$

$y = 2$, $x = 8$, so $2 = \frac{k}{\sqrt[3]{8}}$ giving k = 4

So $y = \frac{4}{\sqrt[3]{x}}$

When $x = 27$, $y = \frac{4}{\sqrt[3]{27}} = \frac{4}{3}$

## Quick Test

1. $y$ is directly proportional to $x$. When $y = 9$, $x = 3$
   Work out the value of $y$ when $x = 4$
2. $y$ is indirectly proportional to $x^2$. When $y = 50$, $x = 5$
   Work out the value of $y$ when $x = 3$

# Upper and Lower Bounds

## Limits of Accuracy

Measurements are often rounded values. The actual value will be between the **lower bound** and the **upper bound**. The bounds are sometimes called the **limits of accuracy**.

You can show the limits of accuracy on a number line. For example, 8 cm to the nearest centimetre:

## Discrete Data

**Discrete data** can only take **certain values** within a given range, e.g. number of people and amounts of money.

> ### Example
>
> At a football match, there are 3500 people to the nearest 100. What are the minimum and maximum number of people at the match?
>
> **Solution**
> 3450 is the lowest whole number that rounds to 3500 to the nearest 100.
>
> 3549 is the highest whole number that rounds to 3500 to the nearest 100.
>
> So minimum = 3450 and maximum = 3549

## Continuous Data

**Continuous data** can take **any value** within a given range, e.g. length and time.

> ### Example
>
> A man is 1.8 metres tall to the nearest tenth of a metre.
>
> What is the shortest and tallest he could be?
>
> **Solution**
> 1.75 metres is the smallest possible value.
>
> 1.849 999 999 99... metres is the tallest he could be but 1.85 metres is the upper bound.
>
> So you write 1.75 m $\leqslant$ height of man $<$ 1.85 m

## Calculations using Upper and Lower Bounds

If two rounded values are added, subtracted, multiplied or divided, you can work out the **minimum** and **maximum** value possible by doing the calculations shown in the table.

|  | Minimum Value | Maximum Value |
|---|---|---|
| **Addition** $(x + y)$ | $x_{min} + y_{min}$ | $x_{max} + y_{max}$ |
| **Subtraction** $(x - y)$ | $x_{min} - y_{max}$ | $x_{max} - y_{min}$ |
| **Multiplication** $(x \times y)$ | $x_{min} \times y_{min}$ | $x_{max} \times y_{max}$ |
| **Division** $(x \div y)$ | $x_{min} \div y_{max}$ | $x_{max} \div y_{min}$ |

### Example

A rectangle has sides of 6 cm and 9 cm, to the nearest centimetre.

9 cm

6 cm

**a)** Work out the smallest possible perimeter.

#### Solution

| Problem Solving |
|---|
| Remember that the perimeter of a rectangle = $2l + 2w$, where $l$ = length and $w$ = width. Use the lower bounds for the smallest possible perimeter. |

The smallest possible perimeter uses the lower bounds, 5.5 cm and 8.5 cm.

Smallest possible perimeter is
5.5 + 8.5 + 5.5 + 8.5 = 28 cm

**b)** Work out the largest possible area.

#### Solution

| Problem Solving |
|---|
| Remember that the area of a rectangle = $lw$, where $l$ = length and $w$ = width. Use the upper bounds for the largest possible area. |

The largest possible area uses the upper bounds, 6.5 cm and 9.5 cm.

Largest possible area is 6.5 × 9.5 = 61.75 cm$^2$

## Quick Test

1. Write down the upper and lower bounds for these values:
   **a)** 50 people given to the nearest 10
   **b)** 50 mph given to the nearest mile per hour
   **c)** 50 cm given to the nearest 5 cm

2. A woman runs 400 metres to the nearest metre. She takes 52 seconds to the nearest second. Work out her slowest and fastest possible average speed.

# Recurring Decimals and Surds

## Terminating and Recurring Decimals

A **terminating decimal** is a decimal that has a finite number of digits, e.g. $\frac{1}{2} = 0.5$ or $\frac{1}{4} = 0.25$

A **recurring decimal** has an infinite number of digits in a repeating pattern, e.g. $\frac{1}{3} = 0.333\ 333\ldots$
or $\frac{2}{11} = 0.181\ 818\ldots$

These recurring decimals are written as $0.\dot{3}$
and $0.\dot{1}\dot{8}$

## Converting Fractions into Recurring Decimals

To convert a fraction into a decimal, divide the numerator by the denominator.

### Example 1

Use a calculator to convert $\frac{2}{7}$ into a recurring decimal.

**Solution**

$2 \div 7 = 0.285\ 714\ 285\ 714\ldots$

$\qquad = 0.\dot{2}85\ 71\dot{4}$

### Example 2

Convert $\frac{2}{7}$ into a recurring decimal without using a calculator.

**Solution**

$\qquad 0.2\ 8\ 5\ 7\ 1\ 4\ 2\ldots$

$7\,|\,\overline{2.0^60^40^50^10^30^20\ldots}$

$\qquad = 0.\dot{2}85\ 71\dot{4}$

## Converting Recurring Decimals into Fractions

You may be asked to convert recurring decimals into fractions.

### Example

Convert $0.5\dot{4}$ into a fraction.

**Solution**

**Problem Solving**

Write out the recurring decimal using digits. Identify the number of digits that recur. If $N$ digits recur, multiply the recurring decimal by $10^N$.

Let $x$ be the fraction.

$x = 0.545\ 454\ldots$

$100x = 54.545\ 454\ldots$  ◄ In this case two digits recur, so multiply by $10^2 = 100$

$100x - x = 54.545\ 454\ldots - 0.545\ 454\ldots$

$99x = 54$  ◄ Subtract $x$ to obtain a whole number

$x = \frac{54}{99}$  ◄ Divide both sides by 99

**Terminating decimal • Recurring decimal**

## Surds

A **rational number** is a number of the form $\frac{a}{b}$ where $a$ and $b$ are integers.

**Surds** are numbers left in **root form** that will **not simplify** to a rational number. $\sqrt{2}$ and $\sqrt[3]{5}$ are examples of surds. You will only need to work with square roots. A surd is an **exact answer**.

---

**Example 1**

Simplify:

**a)** $\sqrt{3} \times \sqrt{3}$

**Solution**

$\sqrt{3} \times \sqrt{3} = 3$

**b)** $\sqrt{75}$

> It will simplify because one factor of 75 is the square number 25

**Solution**

$\sqrt{75} = \sqrt{25 \times 3}$

$= \sqrt{25} \times \sqrt{3}$

$= 5\sqrt{3}$

**c)** $\left(2 + \sqrt{2}\right)^2$

> See *Expanding Brackets and Factorising*, pages 26–27

**Solution**

$\left(2 + \sqrt{2}\right)^2 = \left(2 + \sqrt{2}\right)\left(2 + \sqrt{2}\right)$

> This is the form $a + b\sqrt{2}$

$= 4 + 2\sqrt{2} + 2\sqrt{2} + 2$

$= 6 + 4\sqrt{2}$

---

**Example 2**

Work out the length $x$ in the triangle. Give your answer as a surd.

**Solution**

> **Problem Solving**
> The right-angled triangle is a clue that you will need to use Pythagoras' theorem (see page 64).

$x^2 = 3^2 + 2^2$  ← $c^2 = a^2 + b^2$

$= 9 + 4 = 13$

$x = \sqrt{13}$ cm ← This is an exact value

---

## Rationalising a Denominator

To **rationalise** a denominator is to make the denominator a rational number. To do this, multiply the numerator and denominator by the surd.

**Example**

Rationalise the denominator and simplify $\frac{10}{\sqrt{5}}$

**Solution**

$\frac{10}{\sqrt{5}} = \frac{10}{\sqrt{5}} \times \frac{\sqrt{5}}{\sqrt{5}}$

$= \frac{10\sqrt{5}}{5}$  ← Cancel the 10 and the 5

$= 2\sqrt{5}$

---

### Quick Test

1. Change these fractions into decimals:
   a) $\frac{2}{5}$  b) $\frac{4}{9}$  c) $\frac{3}{13}$

2. Change $0.2\dot{1}$ into a fraction in its simplest form.

3. a) Simplify $\sqrt{18}$

   b) Write $\left(3 + \sqrt{5}\right)^2$ in the form $a + b\sqrt{5}$

4. Rationalise the denominator and simplify $\frac{8}{\sqrt{2}}$

---

# Basic Algebra

## Algebra Facts

You need to know the meaning of these words:

- A **variable** is a letter that is used to represent any number, e.g. $x$ or $y$.
- An **expression** is a combination of variables with numbers, e.g. $2x + 3y$ or $\frac{x}{2} + 1$
- An **equation** contains an equals sign and at least one variable, e.g. $2x + 5 = 16$ or $x + 3y = 7$
- A **formula** also contains an equals sign but is a rule connecting more than one variable, e.g. $A = \pi r^2$ or $s = \frac{d}{t}$
- An **identity** contains an identity sign and is true for all values, e.g. $x + x \equiv 2x$ or $(x + 5)^2 \equiv x^2 + 10x + 25$
- A **term** is one part of an expression, equation, formula or identity, e.g. $2x - 3y + 4$ has the three terms $2x$, $-3y$ and $+4$.
- An **integer** is a whole number.

> **Example**
>
> You are given that $n$ is a positive integer.
>
> Show clearly why $2n + 1$ is always odd.
>
> **Solution**
>
> | Problem Solving |
> | --- |
> | It's not enough to simply substitute values for $n$. This would only show it's true for those particular values. |
>
> An integer is a whole number.
>
> 2 × any positive whole number is always even. ← Multiples of 2 are even
>
> Even + 1 = odd
>
> So $2n + 1$ is always odd.

## Collecting Like Terms

**Like terms** are terms with the same variable.
Here are some examples:

- $2x$ and $3x$
- $2xy$ and $3xy$
- $x^2$ and $4x^2$

To **simplify** an expression, you **collect like terms**.

$a + a + a = 3a$

> **Example**
>
> a) Simplify $3x + 4x$
>
> **Solution**
> $3x + 4x$ simplifies to $7x$
>
> b) Simplify fully $x^2 + 4x - 7x + 3x^2$
>
> **Solution**
> $x^2 + 4x - 7x + 3x^2$
> simplifies to $4x^2 - 3x$ ← $x^2 + 3x^2 = 4x^2$ and $+ 4x - 7x = -3x$
>
> c) Simplify $xy + 3yx - 2xy$
>
> **Solution**
> $xy + 3yx - 2xy$
> simplifies to $2xy$ ← Note that $yx$ is the same as $xy$

## Substitution

**Substitution** is replacing variables (letters) with numbers.

> **Example**
>
> If $x = 2$, $y = -3$ and $z = 0$, work out the value of:
>
> **a)** $5x - 4y$
>
> **Solution**
>
> $5x - 4y = 5 \times 2 - 4 \times -3$ ← Substitute the values for $x$ and $y$
>
> $= 10 + 12$ ← Show your working out
>
> $= 22$
>
> **b)** $xyz$
>
> **Solution**
>
> $xyz = 2 \times -3 \times 0$ ← Substitute the values for $x$, $y$ and $z$
>
> $= 0$
>
> **c)** $y^2 - x$
>
> **Solution**
>
> $y^2 - x = (-3)^2 - 2$ ← Use brackets as the minus sign is also squared
>
> $= 9 - 2$ ← Show your working out
>
> $= 7$

## Changing the Subject of a Formula

To **change the subject** of a formula:

1. collect all subject terms to one side of the formula
2. collect everything else to the other side
3. factorise (see page 26) if possible
4. rearrange to leave the subject on its own.

> **Example 1**
>
> Make $x$ the subject of $y = 3x + 2$
>
> **Solution**
>
> $y - 2 = 3x$ ← Collect the subject term ($3x$) on one side and everything else on the other by subtracting 2 from both sides
>
> $\dfrac{y - 2}{3} = x$ ← Divide by 3 to leave the subject ($x$) on its own

> **Example 2**
>
> Make $P$ the subject of $A = P + \dfrac{PRT}{100}$
>
> **Solution**
>
> $100A = 100P + PRT$ ← It's easier here to multiply by 100 first to remove the fractions
>
> $100A = P(100 + RT)$ ← Factorise as the subject $P$ is a common factor
>
> $\dfrac{100A}{100 + RT} = P$ ← Rearrange to leave the subject ($P$) on its own

> **Quick Test**
>
> 1. Simplify each of the following:
>    a) $8x - 3x$
>    b) $2x + 3y - 6x + 4y$
>    c) $4x^2 + 5xy - 6x^2 + 4xy$
>    d) $5x + 4y + 2x - 4y + z - 2z$
> 2. You are given that $x = 4$, $y = -\dfrac{1}{2}$ and $z = -1$. Work out the value of:
>    a) $2x + 6y$
>    b) $3x + y - 4z$
>    c) $xy - yz$
> 3. Make $x$ the subject of:
>    a) $y + 2x = y(6 + x)$
>    b) $y = \dfrac{x + 2}{x - 3}$

# Expanding Brackets and Factorising

## Expanding Brackets

To **expand** or **multiply out** brackets, every term in the bracket is multiplied by the term outside the bracket.

To multiply out two brackets, each term in the second bracket is multiplied by each term in the first bracket. The result is called a **quadratic expression**.

### Example 1

**a)** Multiply out $5(x + 4)$

**Solution**
$5(x + 4) = 5x + 20$

**b)** Expand and simplify $9(x - 3) - 2(3x - 4)$

**Solution**
$9(x - 3) - 2(3x - 4)$

$= 9x - 27 - 6x + 8$ ← Multiply out each bracket separately

$= 3x - 19$ ← Collect like terms

### Example 2

Expand and simplify:

**a)** $(x + 5)(x - 3)$

**Solution**
$(x + 5)(x - 3) = x(x - 3) + 5(x - 3)$

$= x^2 - 3x + 5x - 15$ ← Multiply out each bracket separately

$= x^2 + 2x - 15$ ← Collect like terms

**b)** $(2x - 7)(3x - 1)$

**Solution**
$(2x - 7)(3x - 1) = 2x(3x - 1) - 7(3x - 1)$

$= 6x^2 - 2x - 21x + 7$ ← Multiply out each bracket separately

$= 6x^2 - 23x + 7$

### Example 3

Prove that the square of any odd number is always 1 more than a multiple of 8.

**Solution**

| Problem Solving |
|---|
| Set up an expression using the information given. |

If $n$ is an integer, $2n + 1$ must be odd. ← When you double a whole number and add 1, you will always get an odd number

$(2n + 1)^2$ ← You have set up an expression for the square of any odd number

$= 4n^2 + 2n + 2n + 1$ ← Expand the brackets

$= 4n^2 + 4n + 1$ ← Collect the terms

$= 4n(n + 1) + 1$ ← Factorise the first two terms

$n(n + 1)$ is even so it's a multiple of 2. ← Odd × even or even × odd

So $4n(n + 1)$ is a multiple of 8.

## Factorisation

**Factorisation** is the reverse process of multiplying out brackets. To factorise you have to look for **common factors** in every term.

### Example

Factorise:

**a)** $3x + 6$    **Solution** $3x + 6 = 3(x + 2)$

**b)** $4x^2 + 3x$    **Solution** $4x^2 + 3x = x(4x + 3)$

**c)** $8xy - 6x^2$    **Solution** $8xy - 6x^2 = 2x(4y - 3x)$

$2x$ is the highest common factor of $8xy$ and $-6x^2$

# Expanding Brackets and Factorising

## Factorising Quadratic Expressions

### Expressions of the Form $x^2 + bx + c$

To factorise a quadratic expression of this form:

**1** write out the brackets as $(x \quad )(x \quad )$

**2** use this table to decide the signs in the brackets:

| | $c$ is Positive | $c$ is Negative |
|---|---|---|
| $b$ is Positive | $(x + )(x + )$ | $(x + )(x - )$ |
| $b$ is Negative | $(x - )(x - )$ | $(x + )(x - )$ |

**3** test numbers which multiply together to give $c$ and add together to give $b$.

**Example**

Factorise $x^2 - x - 12$

**Solution**

$(x + )(x - )$ ← $b$ is negative and $c$ is negative

$= (x + 3)(x - 4)$ ← $3 \times -4 = -12$ and $3 + -4 = -1$

Check $(x + 3)(x - 4) = x(x - 4) + 3(x - 4)$

$= x^2 - 4x + 3x - 12$

$= x^2 - x - 12$

### Expressions of the Form $ax^2 + bx + c$

To factorise a quadratic expression of this form:

**1** write out the brackets as $(px \quad )(qx \quad )$ where $pq = a$

**2** use this table to decide the signs in the brackets:

| | $c$ is Positive | $c$ is Negative |
|---|---|---|
| $b$ is Positive | $(px + )(qx + )$ | $(px + )(qx - )$ |
| $b$ is Negative | $(px - )(qx - )$ | $(px + )(qx - )$ |

**3** test numbers which multiply together to give $c$

**4** multiply out all the possible combinations until you find the correct pairing.

**Example**

Factorise $2x^2 + 7x + 3$

**Solution**

$(x + )(2x + )$ ← $pq = 2$, $b$ is positive and $c$ is positive

$= (x + 3)(2x + 1)$

Check $(x + 3)(2x + 1) = x(2x + 1) + 3(2x + 1)$

$= 2x^2 + x + 6x + 3$

$= 2x^2 + 7x + 3$

### Difference of Two Squares

A quadratic expression of the form $a^2 - b^2$ is called a **difference of two squares**, e.g. $x^2 - 25$ or $4x^2 - 49y^2$.

$a^2 - b^2$ factorises as $(a - b)(a + b)$.

**Example 1**

Factorise $4x^2 - 49y^2$

Notice that $4x^2$ is $(2x)^2$ and $49y^2$ is $(7y)^2$ so this is a difference of two squares

**Solution**

$4x^2 - 49y^2 = (2x)^2 - (7y)^2$

$= (2x - 7y)(2x + 7y)$

**Example 2**

Simplify $\frac{9x^2 - 4}{3x^2 + x - 2}$

Factorising the numerator and denominator

Cancelling the common factor $(3x - 2)$

**Solution**

$\frac{9x^2 - 4}{3x^2 + x - 2}$

$= \frac{(3x - 2)(3x + 2)}{(3x - 2)(x + 1)}$

$= \frac{(3x + 2)}{(x + 1)}$

## Quick Test

**1** Multiply out $5(2x + 3)$

**2** Expand and simplify $(x + 3)(x - 5)$

**3** Factorise:

   **a)** $8x^2 - 12x$     **b)** $x^2 - 3x + 2$

   **c)** $3x^2 - 11x - 20$    **d)** $x^2 - 16y^2$

# Linear Equations

## Equations

An **equation** has an unknown value to be worked out. This is called **solving** the equation.

You should already know how to solve **one-step linear equations**.

**Example**

Solve:

a) $x + 4 = 7$  **Solution** $x = 3$ — Subtract 4 from both sides

b) $x - 5 = 11$  **Solution** $x = 16$

c) $2x = 8$  **Solution** $x = 4$

d) $\frac{x}{10} = 3$  **Solution** $x = 30$ — Multiply both sides by 10

## Using the Balance Method to Solve Equations

The sides of an equation should **balance**.
So whatever you do to one side of the equation, you must also do to the other side.

**Example 1**

Solve $\quad 2x + 3 = 11$

**Solution**

$$2x \;(+ 3) = 11$$
$$\quad\; (- 3) \; - 3$$
$$\overline{2x \qquad = 8}$$

Subtract 3 from both sides of the equation to leave just the $x$-term on the left-hand side. Note that +3 and −3 give a zero, shown by the circle

$$\frac{2x}{2} = \frac{8}{2}$$

Divide both sides by 2 to leave just $x$ on the left-hand side

$$x = 4$$

**Example 2**

Solve $\quad 8x - 5 = 4x + 3$

**Solution**

$$8x \;(- 5) = 4x + 3$$
$$\quad\; (+ 5) \qquad\; + 5$$
$$\overline{8x \qquad = (4x) + 8}$$
$$- 4x \qquad\quad (- 4x)$$
$$\overline{4x \qquad = \qquad 8}$$

Add 5 to both sides of the equation to leave just the $x$-term on the left-hand side. Note that −5 and +5 give a zero, shown by the circle

Subtract $4x$ from both sides of the equation to leave just the number 8 on the right-hand side. Note that $4x$ and $-4x$ give a zero, shown by the circle

$$\frac{4x}{4} = \frac{8}{4}$$

Divide both sides by 4 to leave just $x$ on the left-hand side

$$x = 2$$

## Example 3

Solve $6(2x - 1) = 5(2x + 4)$

**Solution**

$$12x - 6 = 10x + 20$$

Multiply out the brackets on both sides

$$12x \; \fbox{$- 6$} = 10x + 20$$
$$\fbox{$+ 6$} \qquad\qquad + 6$$

Add 6 to both sides of the equation to leave just the $x$-term on the left-hand side. Note that −6 and +6 give a zero, shown by the circle

$$12x = 10x + 26$$
$$- 10x \qquad - 10x$$

Subtract $10x$ from both sides of the equation to leave just the number 26 on the right-hand side. Note that $10x$ and $-10x$ give a zero, shown by the circle

$$2x = 26$$

$$\frac{2x}{2} = \frac{26}{2}$$

Divide both sides by 2 to leave just $x$ on the left-hand side

$$x = 13$$

## Example 4

The sum of $x$, $4x$ and $x + 1$ is 43. Work out the value of $x$.

**Solution**

> **Problem Solving**
>
> Always set up an equation to work out the answer. If you use trial and improvement, you may not find the answer. Once you have set up the equation, solve it as normal.

$$x + 4x + x + 1 = 43$$

$$6x + 1 = 43$$
$$- 1 = - 1$$

Subtract 1 from both sides of the equation to leave just the $x$-term on the left-hand side

$$6x = 42$$

$$\frac{6x}{6} = \frac{42}{6}$$

Divide both sides by 6 to leave just $x$ on the left-hand side

$$x = 7$$

## Quick Test

Solve these equations.

1. **a)** $5x - 7 = 8$
   **b)** $7x - 1 = 13$
   **c)** $6x + 5 = 2x$

2. **a)** $3x + 5 = x - 9$
   **b)** $8x - 1 = 3x + 9$
   **c)** $\frac{1}{2}x - 2 = 7 - x$

3. **a)** $6(2x + 1) = 3(x + 11)$
   **b)** $3(2x - 5) = 2(x - 2)$
   **c)** $8(x - 1) = 5(x + 1)$

# Quadratic Equations

## Solving Quadratic Equations by Factorising

To solve a **quadratic equation** by **factorising**:

1. write the equation into the form $ax^2 + bx + c = 0$
2. factorise $ax^2 + bx + c$
3. equate each bracket to zero
4. solve the linear equations.

### Example 1

Solve $x^2 - 5x + 6 = 0$

**Solution**

$x^2 - 5x + 6 = 0$

$(x - 2)(x - 3) = 0$

So $x - 2 = 0$ or $x - 3 = 0$

$x = 2$ or $x = 3$

### Example 2

Solve $2x^2 + 7x - 4 = 0$

**Solution**

$2x^2 + 7x - 4 = 0$

$(2x - 1)(x + 4) = 0$

So $2x - 1 = 0$ or $x + 4 = 0$

$2x = 1$ or $x = -4$

$x = \frac{1}{2}$ or $x = -4$

### Example 3

The solutions of a quadratic equation are $x = 2$ and $x = -4$

Work out the equation.

**Solution**

**Problem Solving**

To obtain the quadratic equation, work backwards from the solutions.

$x = 2$ and $x = -4$

So $x - 2 = 0$ or $x + 4 = 0$ ← Set up the linear equations

So $(x - 2)(x + 4) = 0$ ← Combine the equations to form a quadratic

$x^2 + 2x - 8 = 0$ ← Expand the brackets

## Solving Quadratic Equations by Completing the Square

To **complete the square** of a quadratic equation of the form $x^2 + bx + c = 0$:

1. write the equation into the form $x^2 + bx + c = 0$
2. rewrite $x^2 + bx$ as $(x + \frac{b}{2})^2 - (\frac{b}{2})^2$
3. remember to add $c$ back on
4. solve the equation.

### Example 1

Solve $x^2 - 8x - 6 = 0$ by completing the square.

**Solution**

$x^2 - 8x - 6 = 0$

$(x - 4)^2 - (-4)^2 - 6 = 0$

$(x - 4)^2 - 16 - 6 = 0$

$(x - 4)^2 = 22$ ← Add 16 and 6 to both sides

$x - 4 = \pm\sqrt{22}$ ← Take the square root of both sides

$x = 4 \pm\sqrt{22}$ ← Answer in surd form

$x = 8.69$ or $x = -0.69$ ← Answers given to 2 decimal places

**Key Words**     Quadratic equation • Complete the square

## Example 2

Here is an identity:

$x^2 + 6x - 5 \equiv (x + a)^2 + b$

**a)** Work out the values of $a$ and $b$.

### Solution

**Problem Solving**

To work out $a$ compare the $x$-terms and to work out $b$ compare the constants.

$(x + a)^2 + b$ expanded gives $x^2 + 2ax + a^2 + b$

So $x^2 + 6x - 5 \equiv x^2 + 2ax + a^2 + b$

Comparing the $x$-terms:

$6 = 2a$, so $a = 3$ ← This is called equating coefficients of $x$

Comparing the constants:

$-5 = a^2 + b$

So $-5 = 9 + b$

$b = -14$

**b)** Solve $x^2 + 6x - 5 = 0$

### Solution

$x^2 + 6x - 5 = 0$

So $(x + 3)^2 - 9 - 5 = 0$

$(x + 3)^2 - 14 = 0$

$(x + 3)^2 = 14$ ← Add 14 to both sides

$x + 3 = \pm\sqrt{14}$ ← Take the square root of both sides

$x = -3 \pm\sqrt{14}$ ← Answer in surd form

$x = 0.74$ or $x = -6.74$ ← Answers given to 2 decimal places

## Solving Quadratic Equations by using the Quadratic Formula

Quadratic equations of the form $ax^2 + bx + c = 0$ can be solved using the **quadratic formula**:

$$x = \frac{-b \pm \sqrt{b^2 - 4ac}}{2a}$$

### Quick Test

1. Solve by factorising:
   **a)** $x^2 - 11x + 18 = 0$
   **b)** $3x^2 - 14x - 5 = 0$
2. Solve by completing the square. Give your answer in surd form.
   **a)** $x^2 - 6x + 4 = 0$
   **b)** $x^2 + 3x - 11 = 0$
3. Solve by using the quadratic formula:
   **a)** $2x^2 + x - 8 = 0$
   **b)** $3x^2 - 7x + 1 = 0$

## Example

Solve $5x^2 + 2x - 4 = 0$

Give your answers to 2 decimal places. ← This is a clue that the quadratic will not factorise

### Solution

$a = 5$, $b = 2$, $c = -4$

Substitute for $a$, $b$ and $c$ in the formula

So $x = \dfrac{-(2) \pm \sqrt{(2)^2 - 4 \times (5) \times (-4)}}{2 \times (5)}$

$x = \dfrac{-2 \pm \sqrt{4 + 80}}{10}$

$x = \dfrac{-2 \pm \sqrt{84}}{10}$

$x = \dfrac{-2 + \sqrt{84}}{10}$ or $x = \dfrac{-2 - \sqrt{84}}{10}$

$x = 0.72$ or $x = -1.12$

# Trial and Improvement & Sequences

## Trial and Improvement

You can use **trial and improvement** to solve equations. It involves trying values and improving them to get as close as possible to the solution.

### Example 1

Use trial and improvement to find the solution to $x^3 = 30$. Give your answer to 1 decimal place.

**Solution**

| $x$ | $x^3$ | Comment |
|-----|-------|---------|
| 3 | 27 | Too small |
| 4 | 64 | Too big |
| 3.2 | 32.768 | Too big |
| 3.1 | 29.791 | Too small |
| 3.15 | 31.255 875 | Too big |

Solution between $x = 3$ and $x = 4$

Solution between $x = 3.1$ and $x = 3.2$

The solution is between $x = 3.1$ and $x = 3.15$
So to 1 decimal place, the solution is $x = 3.1$

### Example 2

Show that the equation $x^3 - 12x = 50$ has a solution between 4 and 5.

**Solution**

| Problem Solving |
|-----------------|
| Write the equation with all terms on one side, then complete a table to present your answer clearly and logically. |

$x^3 - 12x - 50 = 0$

| $x$ | $x^3 - 12x - 50$ | Comment |
|-----|------------------|---------|
| 4 | $4^3 - (12 \times 4) - 50 = -34$ | Too small |
| 5 | $5^3 - (12 \times 5) - 50 = 15$ | Too big |

So the solution is between 4 and 5.

## Number Patterns and Sequences

You should be familiar with these number sequences:

- **Odd** numbers:
  1    3    5    7    9    …
- **Even** numbers:
  2    4    6    8    10    …
- **Square** numbers:
  1    4    9    16    25    …
- **Cube** numbers:
  1    8    27    64    125    …

You also need to know the following:
- A **sequence** is a set of numbers with a rule to find each number.
- A **term-to-term rule** is a rule that links one term to the next term, e.g. the term-to-term rule for odd numbers is 'add 2'.
- A **position-to-term rule** is a rule that links the position of the term to the term, e.g. the position-to-term rule for odd numbers is 'double the position number and subtract 1':

| Position | 1 | 2 | 3 | 4 | 5 |
|----------|---|---|---|---|---|
| Term | 1 | 3 | 5 | 7 | 9 |

So the 5th term is $2 \times 5 - 1 = 9$

## The $n$th Term of a Sequence

The $n$th term of a sequence is a formula for the position-to-term rule, e.g. the formula for the $n$th term for odd numbers would be $2n - 1$.

N.B. A common mistake is to give the term-to-term rule as the $n$th term.

**Key Words**      Trial and improvement • Sequence • Term-to-term rule • Position-to-term rule

## Example 1

Work out the $n$th term of this sequence:

7   10   13   16   19   …

**Solution**

The term-to-term rule is 'add 3':

So the sequence is linked to the 3 times table.

So the $n$th term will be of the form $3n + c$.

When $n = 1$:    $3 \times 1 + c = 7$, so $c = 4$

So the $n$th term is $3n + 4$.

## Example 2

Work out the $n$th term of this sequence:

11   9   7   5   …

**Solution**

The term-to-term rule is 'subtract 2':

So the sequence is linked to the 2 times table.

So the $n$th term will be of the form $-2n + c$.

When $n = 1$:    $-2 \times 1 + c = 11$, so $c = 13$

So the $n$th term is $-2n + 13$ or $13 - 2n$.

## Quick Test

1  Use trial and improvement to find a solution to 1 decimal place.
   a) $x^3 = 20$     b) $x^3 - 10x + 6 = 0$

2  For each sequence:
   i)   write down the next two terms
   ii)  work out the $n$th term
   iii) work out the 20th term.
   a) 5   8   11   14   17   …
   b) 10   14   18   22   26   …

## Example 3

A café has tables to seat 4 people. When put together 2 tables can seat 6 people, and so on.

How many people can sit at $n$ tables in this way?

**Solution**

| Position | 1 | 2 | 3 |
|---|---|---|---|
| Term | 4 | 6 | 8 |

The term-to-term rule is 'add 2'.

So the $n$th term will be of the form $2n + c$.

When $n = 1$:    $2 \times 1 + c = 4$, so $c = 2$

So the $n$th term is $2n + 2$.

The number of people at $n$ tables is $2n + 2$.

## Example 4

Jack says that 87 is in this sequence:

6   13   20   27   34   …

Is he correct? You must show your working.

**Solution**

**Problem Solving**

To test if a number is part of a sequence, work out the $n$th term and test if an integer value for $n$ gives that number.

The term-to-term rule is 'add 7':

So the $n$th term will be of the form $7n + c$.

When $n = 1$:    $7 \times 1 + c = 6$, so $c = -1$

So the $n$th term is $7n - 1$.

Solving $7n - 1 = 87$ gives $n = 12.57$

So 87 is between the 12th and 13th terms.

> The 12th term is $7 \times 12 - 1 = 83$ and the 13th term is $7 \times 13 - 1 = 90$

Jack isn't correct.

# Straight Line Graphs

## Linear Graphs

A **linear graph** is a straight line graph, e.g. $y = x$, $y = 2x + 3$, $x + y = 5$, etc.

To draw the graph:

1. choose three values for $x$ (pick any three easy values in the range of the graph – the highest and lowest are often sensible points to use)
2. work out the corresponding $y$-values
3. plot the points on a grid
4. draw a straight, ruled line through the points.

### Example 1

Draw the graph of $y = 2x + 3$ for values of $x$ from −2 to 2.

**Solution**

Choosing $x = -2$, $x = 0$ and $x = 2$ ← Choose three values for $x$

When $x = -2$
$y = 2 \times -2 + 3 = -1$ ← Work out each corresponding $y$-value

When $x = 0$
$y = 2 \times 0 + 3 = 3$

When $x = 2$
$y = 2 \times 2 + 3 = 7$

| $x$ | −2 | 0 | 2 |
|-----|-----|-----|-----|
| $y$ | −1 | 3 | 7 |

This gives the points to plot on the grid: (−2, −1), (0, 3) and (2, 7)

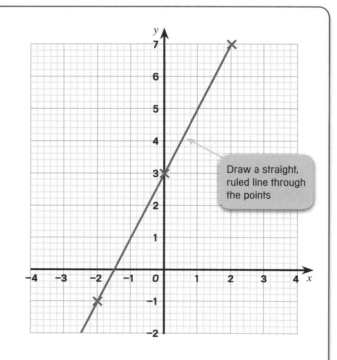

Draw a straight, ruled line through the points

### Example 2

Draw the graph of $x + y = 5$ for values of $x$ from 0 to 5.

**Solution**

Choosing $x = 0$, $x = 2$ and $x = 5$ ← Choose three values for $x$

When $x = 0$, $y = 5$
When $x = 2$, $y = 3$ ← Work out each corresponding $y$-value
When $x = 5$, $y = 0$

| $x$ | 0 | 2 | 5 |
|-----|-----|-----|-----|
| $y$ | 5 | 3 | 0 |

This gives the points to plot on the grid: (0, 5), (2, 3) and (5, 0)

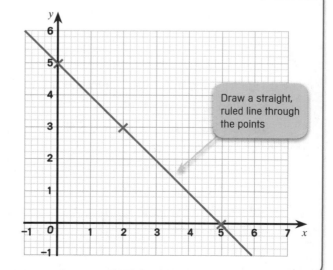

Draw a straight, ruled line through the points

## Gradient

**Gradient** is a measure of the amount a line slopes.
To work out the gradient of a straight line:

1. choose two points on the line and join them
2. draw a right-angled triangle, using the line already drawn as the hypotenuse
3. use the formula:

> **Gradient** = $\dfrac{\textbf{distance up the triangle}}{\textbf{distance across the triangle}}$
>
> or
>
> **Gradient** = $\dfrac{\textbf{difference of } y\textbf{-coordinates}}{\textbf{difference of } x\textbf{-coordinates}}$

Remember the following about lines and their gradients:

- A line sloping up from left to right has a **positive** gradient and a line sloping down from left to right has a **negative** gradient.
- Lines that are **parallel** have the same gradient.
- Lines that are **perpendicular** have gradients that are negative reciprocals of each other, e.g. 2 and $-\frac{1}{2}$ or $\frac{3}{4}$ and $-\frac{4}{3}$. (The product of the gradients = −1 if they're perpendicular.)

### Example

Work out the gradient of these straight lines.

a)

**Solution**

Gradient $= \dfrac{\text{distance up the triangle}}{\text{distance across the triangle}} = \dfrac{4}{2} = 2$

b)

Negative gradient as the line slopes down from left to right

**Solution**

Gradient $= \dfrac{\text{distance up the triangle}}{\text{distance across the triangle}} = -\dfrac{1}{5}$

## $y = mx + c$

Equations of straight lines are often written in the form **$y = mx + c$**, where:

- $m$ is the gradient
- $c$ is the $y$-intercept.

The $y$-intercept is the point where the line crosses the $y$-axis.

### Quick Test

1. Work out the gradient and the coordinates of the $y$-intercept of $2y = 3x + 6$
2. Which of these lines are parallel and which are perpendicular?

   $y = 3x + 1$      $x = 3y + 1$

   $6x - 2y = 9$      $3x + y = 4$

### Example

Write down the gradient and the coordinates of the $y$-intercept in each case.

a) $y = 3x + 2$

**Solution**

Gradient = 3, $y$-intercept is (0, 2)

b) $x + 2y = 5$

**Solution**

Rearranging the equation $x + 2y = 5$ gives:

**Problem Solving**

Write the equation in the form $y = mx + c$

$y = -0.5x + 2.5$ ← Divide both sides by 2

Gradient = −0.5, $y$-intercept is (0, 2.5)

# Linear Inequalities

## Inequality Symbols

**Inequalities** use the symbols:
- $<$ to mean 'less than'
- $>$ to mean 'greater than'
- $\leqslant$ to mean 'less than or equal to'
- $\geqslant$ to mean 'greater than or equal to'.

## Inequalities on a Number Line

The solution to an inequality can be shown on a **number line** using open circles (O) and closed circles (●):

### Example

Show each of these inequalities on a number line:

**a)** $x < 1$

**Solution**

**b)** $x > 4$

**Solution**

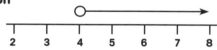

**c)** $x \leqslant 1$

**Solution**

**d)** $x \geqslant 4$

**Solution**

**e)** $-2 \leqslant x < 5$

**Solution**

## Solving Linear Inequalities

When solving a **linear inequality**:
- use the same techniques as when solving an equation
- always collect terms so that the $x$-term has a positive coefficient
- never replace the inequality symbol with an equals sign.

## Example

**a)** Solve $3x - 3 \geqslant x + 7$

**Solution**

$3x - 3 \geqslant x + 7$

$2x - 3 \geqslant 7$ ← Subtract $x$ from both sides

$2x \geqslant 10$ ← Add 3 to both sides

$x \geqslant 5$ ← Divide both sides by 2

**b)** Solve $-2x > 6$

**Solution**

$-2x > 6$

$-6 - 2x > 0$ ← Subtract 6 from both sides

$-6 > 2x$ ← Add $2x$ to both sides

$-3 > x$ or $x < -3$ ← If $-3$ is greater than $x$, then $x$ is less than $-3$

**c)** Work out the integers that satisfy $6 < 3x \leqslant 12$

**Solution**

$6 < 3x \leqslant 12$

$2 < x \leqslant 4$ ← Divide through by 3

3 and 4 satisfy the inequality.

Integers are the whole numbers that satisfy the inequality

## Representing Inequalities on a Graph

A linear inequality can be shown by a region on a graph. The region will lie on one side of the straight line graph for the corresponding equation, e.g.:

- $x < 3$ is the region to the left of the line $x = 3$
- $y \geqslant 4$ is the region above and including the line $y = 4$

You should also know the following:

- For $x <$ or $x >$ a dotted line is used to show that the points on the line are **not** included.
- For $x \leqslant$ or $x \geqslant$ a solid line is used to show that the points on the line are included.

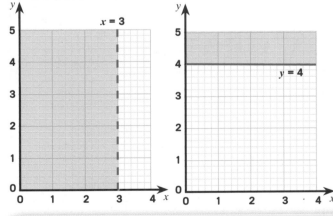

## Example

Show graphically the region, R, that satisfies $x \leqslant 2$, $y \geqslant x$ and $y < 2x$

**Solution**

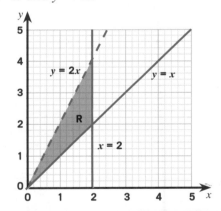

Check your answer by choosing a point in the region and testing that it satisfies all the inequalities

For example, (1.5, 2.5) is in the region marked and $x = 1.5$, $y = 2.5$ obeys all three inequalities.

$x \leqslant 2$, $y \geqslant x$ and $y < 2x$ ← $1.5 < 2, 2.5 > 1.5$ and $2.5 < 3$

## Quick Test

1. Show each inequality on a number line:   **a)** $x \leqslant 3$   **b)** $0 < x \leqslant 4$
2. Solve these inequalities:   **a)** $2x - 8 > 0$   **b)** $2(x + 3) \geqslant 9$
3. Show graphically the region, R, that satisfies $x > 1$, $x \leqslant 2$, $y \geqslant x + 1$ and $y < 4$

# Simultaneous Equations

## Solving Simultaneous Equations

To solve a pair of **simultaneous equations** is to find the pair (or pairs) of solutions that satisfy both equations.

## Elimination and Substitution Methods

To solve by **eliminating** variables, follow these steps:

**1** Match the **coefficients** of one of the variables.

**2** Eliminate this variable by adding or subtracting the equations.

**3** Solve the linear equation in the remaining variable.

**4** Substitute this value back into one of the original equations.

**5** Solve this linear equation in the remaining variable.

**6** Check that your solutions satisfy both the original equations.

To solve by **substitution**, follow these steps:

**1** Rearrange one equation into the form $y = \ldots$ or $x = \ldots$

**2** Substitute for $y$ or $x$ in the other equation.

**3** Solve the equation in the remaining variable.

**4** Substitute this value back into the rearranged equation.

**5** Solve this linear equation in the remaining variable.

**6** Check that your solutions satisfy both the original equations.

### Example

Solve the simultaneous equations $3x + 2y = 7$ and $x - y = -1$

**Solution**

$3x + 2y = 7$

$x - y = -1$ ← To match the coefficients of $y$, multiply this equation by 2

$3x + 2y = 7$
$2x - 2y = -2$ ← To eliminate $y$, add the equations, i.e. **different** signs: **add**

$5x = 5$ ← Divide both sides by 5

$x = 1$

$3 + 2y = 7$ ← Substitute back into the first equation

$2y = 4$ ← Subtract 3 from both sides

$y = 2$

Check:

$3x + 2y = 7 \qquad 3 + 4 = 7\ \checkmark$

$x - y = -1 \qquad 1 - 2 = -1\ \checkmark$

### Example

Solve the simultaneous equations $5x + 3y = 12$ and $3x + 2y = 7$

**Solution**

$5x = 12 - 3y$ ← Subtract $3y$ from both sides of $5x + 3y = 12$

$x = \dfrac{12 - 3y}{5}$ ← Divide by 5

$3\left(\dfrac{12 - 3y}{5}\right) + 2y = 7$ ← Substitute for $x$ in the equation $3x + 2y = 7$

$3(12 - 3y) + 10y = 35$ ← Multiply both sides by 5

$36 - 9y + 10y = 35$ ← Expand the bracket

$y = -1$ ← Collect terms and subtract 36 from both sides

So $x = \dfrac{12 - 3(-1)}{5}$ ← Substitute $y = -1$ into the equation $x = \dfrac{12 - 3y}{5}$

$x = 3$

Check:

$5x + 3y = 12 \qquad 15 - 3 = 12\ \checkmark$

$3x + 2y = 7 \qquad 9 - 2 = 7\ \checkmark$

**Key Words**     Simultaneous equations • Elimination • Substitution

# Simultaneous Equations

## Other Simultaneous Equations

Use the substitution method to solve simultaneous equations
with one linear and one quadratic or of the form $x^2 + y^2 = r^2$

### Example

Solve the simultaneous equations $y = 3 - x$ and
$x^2 + y^2 = 5$

**Solution**

$$x^2 + (3 - x)^2 = 5$$ ← Substitute $y = 3 - x$ into the equation $x^2 + y^2 = 5$

$$x^2 + 9 - 6x + x^2 = 5$$ ← Expand the bracket

$$2x^2 - 6x + 4 = 0$$ ← Collect terms to one side

$$x^2 - 3x + 2 = 0$$ ← Divide both sides by 2

$$(x - 1)(x - 2) = 0$$ ← Factorise

$$x = 1 \text{ or } x = 2$$

When $x = 1$, $y = 2$ and
when $x = 2$, $y = 1$ ← Substitute both the $x$-values into $y = 3 - x$ to find corresponding $y$-values

## Solving Simultaneous Equations Graphically

To solve simultaneous equations graphically:

1. draw the graphs of the two equations
2. the solutions are the point(s) of intersection.

### Example 1

Solve $x + y = 5$ and $2x + y = 7$

**Solution**

Point of intersection is (2, 3)

The solutions are $x = 2$ and $y = 3$

Check: $x + y = 5$    $2 + 3 = 5$ ✓
        $2x + y = 7$    $4 + 3 = 7$ ✓

### Example 2

Solve graphically the simultaneous equations
$y - x = 4$ and $y = 2x^2$

**Solution**

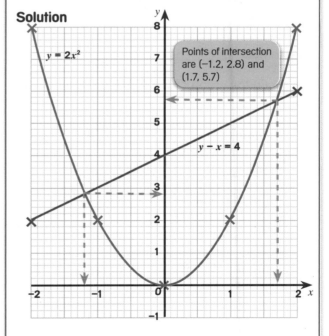

Points of intersection are (−1.2, 2.8) and (1.7, 5.7)

The solutions are $x = -1.2$, $y = 2.8$ and $x = 1.7$, $y = 5.7$

Check: Approximate answers as read from the graph

$y - x = 4$    $2.8 - -1.2 = 4$ and $5.7 - 1.7 = 4$ ✓
$y = 2x^2$    $2(-1.2)^2 = 2.88$ and $2(1.7)^2 = 5.78$ ✓

## Quick Test

1. Solve $4x + 3y = 23$ and $3x - 2y = 13$
2. Solve $y = x - 3$ and $x^2 + y^2 = 17$

# Harder Equations and Graphs

## Harder Algebraic Equations

To achieve the highest grades, you need to be able to solve harder algebraic equations.

**Example**

Solve $\dfrac{3}{2x-1} - \dfrac{4}{3x-1} = 1$

**Solution**

$$\frac{3(3x-1)}{(2x-1)(3x-1)} - \frac{4(2x-1)}{(2x-1)(3x-1)} = \frac{(2x-1)(3x-1)}{(2x-1)(3x-1)}$$
Obtaining a common denominator

$$3(3x-1) - 4(2x-1) = (2x-1)(3x-1)$$
Equating the numerator

$$9x - 3 - 8x + 4 = 6x^2 - 2x - 3x + 1$$
Expanding brackets

$$0 = 6x^2 - 6x$$
Collecting like terms

$$0 = 6x(x-1)$$
Factorising

So $x = 0$ or $x = 1$

## Quadratic Graphs

A **quadratic graph** is a curved graph

 or ∩.

To draw a quadratic graph:

1. complete a table of values
2. plot the points and draw a smooth curve.

**Example**

**a)** Draw the graph of $y = 2x^2 - x - 3$ for values of $x$ from −1 to 2.

**Solution**

| $x$ | −1 | 0 | 1 | 2 |
|-----|----|---|---|---|
| $2x^2$ | 2 | 0 | 2 | 8 |
| $-x$ | 1 | 0 | −1 | −2 |
| $-3$ | −3 | −3 | −3 | −3 |
| $y$ | 0 | −3 | −2 | 3 |

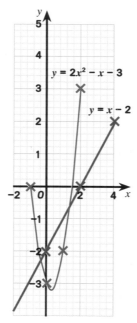

**b)** Use the graph to solve $2x^2 - x - 3 = 0$

**Solution**

$x = -1$ and $x = 1.5$ ← Read off at the points where $y = 0$

**c)** Use the graph to solve $2x^2 - 2x - 1 = 0$

**Solution**

The graph drawn is $y = 2x^2 - x - 3$

The equation to solve is $0 = 2x^2 - 2x - 1$

$$\begin{array}{r} y = 2x^2 - x - 3 \\ 0 = 2x^2 - 2x - 1 \\ \hline y = x - 2 \end{array}$$

Subtract the equations

Draw the line $y = x - 2$ on the graph

This gives solutions $x = -0.4$ and $x = 1.4$

Read off at the points of intersection

Quadratic graph

## Graphs of Cubic, Reciprocal and Exponential Functions

You need to know the following:

- A **cubic** function is of the form
  $y = ax^3 + bx^2 + cx + d$,
  e.g. $y = x^3$ or $y = 2x^3 + 4x + 3$

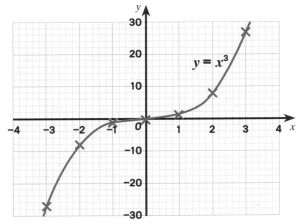

- A **reciprocal** function is of the form $y = \frac{k}{x}$ with $x \neq 0$, e.g. $y = \frac{1}{x}$ or $y = \frac{3}{x}$

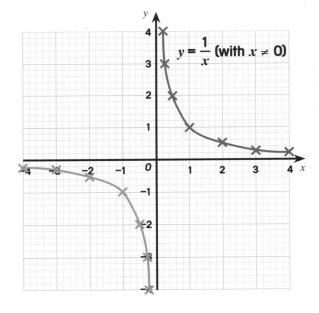

- An **exponential** function is of the form $y = k^x$, e.g. $y = 2^x$ or $y = 3^x$

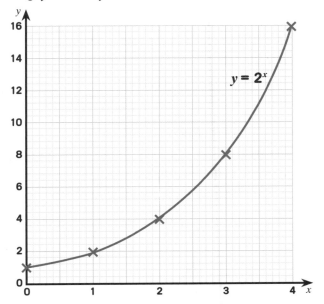

You'll need to plot these types of graphs from a table of values.

### Quick Test

1. Draw the graph of $y = x^2 - 2x - 2$ for values of $x$ from $-2$ to 4.

2. Sketch the graphs of:
   a) $y = x^3$
   b) $y = \frac{1}{x}$
   c) $y = 2^x$

# Trigonometrical Graphs and Transformations

## Graphs of Trigonometrical Functions

Here are the graphs of $y = \sin x$ and $y = \cos x$ for values of $x$ from $-360°$ to $+360°$.

The graph of $y = \sin x$:
- is **cyclic** (the shape repeats indefinitely in both directions)
- has line symmetry about $x = 90°$
- has rotational symmetry about $(180°, 0)$.

The graph of $y = \cos x$:
- is **cyclic**
- has line symmetry about $x = 0°$
- has rotational symmetry about $(90°, 0)$.

You'll need to plot graphs of these types from a table of values.

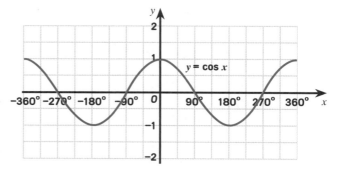

---

### Example

Given that cos 60 = 0.5, use the graph $y = \cos x$ to work out:

**a)** cos 300°

**Solution**

> **Problem Solving**
> Use the symmetrical properties of the graph. In this case use line symmetry with mirror line $x = 180°$

$y = \cos x$ has line symmetry about $x = 180°$ so cos 300° = 0.5

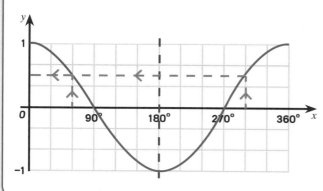

**b)** cos 120°

**Solution**

> **Problem Solving**
> Use the symmetrical properties of the graph. In this case use rotational symmetry about $(90°, 0)$.

$y = \cos x$ has rotational symmetry about $(90°, 0)$ so cos 120° = −0.5

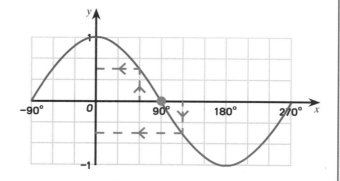

---

**Key Words**      Cyclic

# Trigonometrical Graphs and Transformations

## Transformations of Graphs

The notation $y = f(x)$ is used to represent any graph where $f(x)$ is any **function** of $x$.

From a graph of $y = f(x)$, you'll need to draw the graphs of:

- $y = f(x) + a$ ⟶ A translation of $y = f(x)$ by the **vector** $\binom{0}{a}$
- $y = f(x + a)$ ⟶ A translation of $y = f(x)$ by the vector $\binom{-a}{0}$
- $y = af(x)$ ⟶ A stretch of $y = f(x)$, scale factor $a$ in the $y$-direction
- $y = f(ax)$ ⟶ A stretch of $y = f(x)$, scale factor $\frac{1}{a}$ in the $x$-direction
- $y = -f(x)$ ⟶ A reflection of $y = f(x)$ in the $x$-axis
- $y = f(-x)$ ⟶ A reflection of $y = f(x)$ in the $y$-axis.

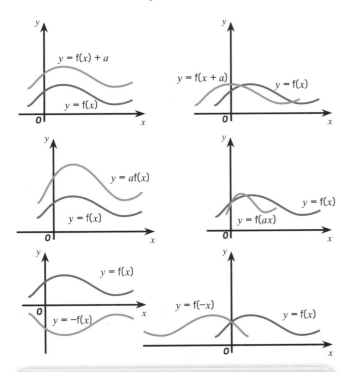

## Quick Test

1. Sketch the graph of $y = \sin x$
2. Describe the transformation of the graph $y = \sin x$ to $y = \sin(x - 90°)$

### Example

The diagram shows the graph of $y = \sin x$ for values of $x$ from $0°$ to $360°$.

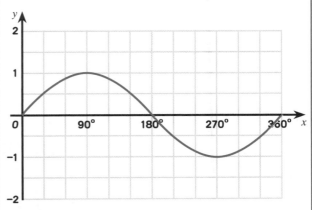

Draw the graphs of:

**a)** $y = 1 + \sin x$

**Solution**

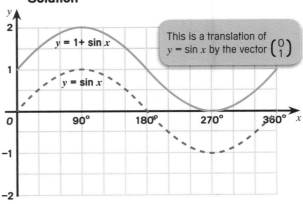

This is a translation of $y = \sin x$ by the vector $\binom{0}{1}$

**b)** $y = 2 \sin x$

**Solution**

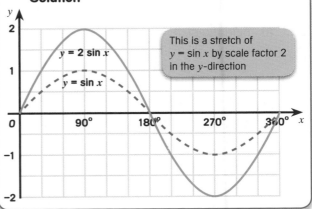

This is a stretch of $y = \sin x$ by scale factor 2 in the $y$-direction

# Exam Practice Questions

You may wish to answer these questions on a separate piece of paper so that you can show full working out, which you will be expected to do in the exam.

Questions labelled with an asterisk (*) are ones where the quality of your written communication (QWC) will be assessed.

 **1.** **a)** Solve $8(1 + 4x) - 4(x + 3) = 0$ **(3)**

      **b)** Solve $\frac{y}{2} - 5 = 11$ **(2)**

**\*2.** Matt wants a new fridge. Three shops have these adverts for the fridge he wants.

Matt wants to pay as little as possible.

From which shop should he buy the fridge?

Show clearly how you get your answer. **(6)**

 **3.** The $n$th term of a sequence is $n^2 + 5$.

      **a)** Find the sixth term of the sequence. **(2)**

      **b)** Is the number 125 a term in the sequence? **(2)**

      Give reasons for your answer.

**\*4.** Abby and Jude share £84 in the ratio 7 : 5

Abby says that she gets £15 more than Jude.

Is she correct? You must show your working out clearly. **(4)**

**5.** Mr Smith bought a new car for £16 500 in January 2008.

He sold it for £6900 in January 2011.

   **a)** Work out the average annual depreciation of the car. **(2)**

   **b)** Estimate the value of the car in January 2012. **(2)**

**6.**   **a)** Work out the least common multiple (LCM) of 9 and 15. **(3)**

   **b)** Work out the highest common factor (HCF) of 36 and 60. **(3)**

**7.**   **a)** Express 42 as a product of prime factors. **(2)**

   **b)** Express $42^2$ as a product of prime factors. **(1)**

**8.** Jack has £5 more than Kylie.

Kylie has half as much as Liam.

Liam has £$x$.

Jack and Kylie give their money to Liam.

Liam now has £20.

   **a)** Show that $x + \frac{x}{2} + \frac{x}{2} + 5 = 20$ **(2)**

   **\*b)** How much did Liam have to start with? **(3)**

# Exam Practice Questions

 **9.**    **a)**   Work out $2\frac{1}{4} + 1\frac{2}{3}$        **(2)**

         **b)**   Work out $3\frac{1}{3} \times 1\frac{1}{2}$        **(3)**

**10.**   Clare spent £168 on her monthly shop. This was 20% more than last month.

How much was her monthly shop last month?        **(3)**

 **11.**   **a)**   Factorise fully $8xy - 12y^2$        **(2)**

        **b)**   Factorise $2x^2 - 5x - 3$        **(2)**

**12.**   Harry earned £15 000 last year. He does not pay tax on the first £5040.

Kim earned £14 400 last year. She does not pay tax on the first £8100.

They both pay tax on 20% of the rest of their earnings.

    **\*a)** Who pays the most tax and by how much?        **(4)**

    **\*b)** Who takes home the most pay and by how much?        **(2)**

 **13.**   **a)**   Write down the value of $8^{\frac{1}{3}}$        **(1)**

        **b)**   Work out the value of $9^{\frac{3}{2}}$        **(2)**

 **14.**   **a)**   The Sun measures 1.4 million kilometres across. Write this as a number in standard form.    **(1)**

        **b)**   Light travels at $3 \times 10^8$ metres per second. Write this as an ordinary number.    **(1)**

**15.** Work out the equation of a line that is perpendicular to the line $y = 3x - 2$ and passes through the point (0, 4). **(3)**

**16.** The diagram shows the graph of $y = x^2$

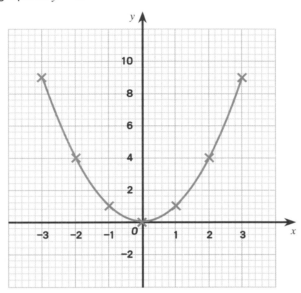

a) On the same grid sketch the graph of $y = x^2 - 2$ **(1)**

b) Write down the coordinates of the vertex of the curve with equation $y = (x + 1)^2$ **(1)**

**\*17.** In an electrical circuit, the current ($I$) is indirectly proportional to the resistance ($R$).

When $I$ = 10 amps, $R$ = 24 ohms

Explain what happens to the current when the resistance doubles.

Show working to support your answer. **(4)**

**18.** a) Write $(3 + \sqrt{5})^2$ in the form $a + b\sqrt{5}$ **(2)**

b) Rationalise the denominator and simplify $\dfrac{10}{\sqrt{2}}$ **(2)**

# Angles and Parallel Lines

## Angle Facts

**Acute angles** are less than 90°.

**Obtuse angles** are between 90° and 180°.

**Reflex angles** are between 180° and 360°.

Angles **on a straight line** add up to **180°**.

$$a + b + c = 180°$$

Angles **at a point** add up to **360°**.

$$a + b + c + d = 360°$$

**Vertically opposite** angles are **equal**.

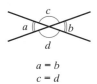

$$a = b$$
$$c = d$$

## Parallel Lines

**Alternate angles** are equal.

**Corresponding angles** are equal.

**Allied angles** add up to 180°.

$$c + d = 180°$$

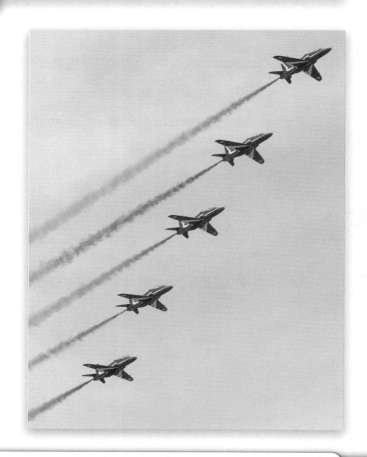

**Key Words**     Acute angle • Obtuse angle • Reflex angle • Alternate angles

## Example 1

Work out the value of $x$.

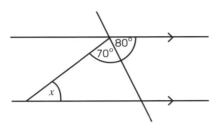

**Problem Solving**

Because there are parallel lines, look out for any alternate or corresponding angles.

**Solution A**

Filling in the missing angle on the straight line gives 30°.

$x$ and 30° are alternate angles, so $x = 30°$

**Solution B**

The other angle in the triangle and 80° are alternate angles.

Angles in a triangle add up to 180°, so $x$ is 180° − 70° − 80° = 30°

## Example 2

Show that $AC$ is parallel to $DG$.

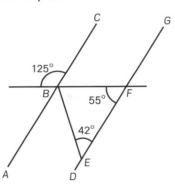

**Solution**

**Problem Solving**

Mark any missing angles you know on the diagram.

Angle $CBF$ is 180° − 125° = 55° ← Angles on a straight line

Angle $CBF$ = angle $BFE$, so they are alternate angles on parallel lines $AC$ and $DG$.

N.B. You don't use the angle of 42° to answer the question.

## Quick Test

 **1** In each part, work out the value of $x$.
Give reasons for your answers.

a)

b)

c)

# Angles of Polygons

## Polygon Facts

You should know the following:

- A **polygon** is a shape made from straight sides, e.g. a **triangle**, a **quadrilateral**, a **pentagon**, and so on.
- **Interior angles** are the angles inside a polygon.
- **Exterior angles** are formed by extending one side of a polygon as shown in the diagram below.
- A **vertex** is a point where two sides meet, i.e. a corner.

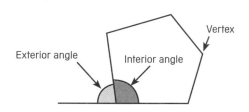

At any vertex:

> **Interior angle + exterior angle = 180°**

Polygons can be divided into triangles. This hexagon has been divided into four triangles. So the sum of its interior angles is:

4 × 180° = 720°

> **Sum of interior angles of any polygon** = $\begin{pmatrix} \text{number of} \\ \text{sides} - 2 \end{pmatrix}$ × 180°

| Name | Triangle | Quadrilateral | Pentagon | Hexagon | Octagon | Decagon |
|---|---|---|---|---|---|---|
| Number of Sides | 3 | 4 | 5 | 6 | 8 | 10 |
| Sum of Interior Angles | 180° | 360° | 540° | 720° | 1080° | 1440° |

## Regular Polygons

A **regular polygon** has:
- all sides of equal length
- all interior angles of equal size
- all exterior angles of equal size
- line symmetry, e.g. a regular hexagon has six sides and six lines of symmetry
- rotational symmetry, e.g. a regular hexagon has rotational symmetry of order 6.

Imagine you are walking around the edge of a regular hexagon. Each time you turn at a vertex, you turn through the exterior angle. To return to the start, you have turned through all six exterior angles and you have turned through 360°.

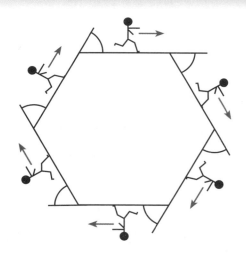

So:

> **Number of sides × exterior angle = 360°**
>
> or
>
> **Exterior angle** = $\dfrac{360°}{\text{number of sides}}$

Polygon • Interior angle • Exterior angle • Vertex • Regular polygon

## Example 1

**a)** Work out the size of each exterior angle of a regular pentagon.

**Solution**

A regular pentagon has five sides.

Exterior angle of a regular pentagon is:

$\frac{360°}{5} = 72°$

**b)** Work out the size of each interior angle of a regular pentagon.

**Solution**

Interior angle + exterior angle = 180°

Interior angle of a regular pentagon is:
180° − 72° = 108°

## Quick Test

① Work out the size of the interior and exterior angles of these regular shapes:

**a)** Octagon      **b)** Decagon

## Example 2

The diagram shows a regular hexagon *ABCDEF*. Work out the size of the angle marked $x$.

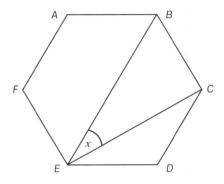

**Solution**

> **Problem Solving**
>
> Break this type of question into several steps. First find the exterior angle and use this to find the interior angle. Then use properties of isosceles triangles.

Exterior angle of a regular hexagon is:

$\frac{360°}{6} = 60°$

Interior angle + exterior angle = 180°

Interior angle of a regular hexagon is:
180° − 60° = 120°

So angle *FED* = 120°

*EB* bisects angle *FED*.

So angle *FEB* is $\frac{120°}{2} = 60°$

Triangle *EDC* is isosceles.

So angle *DEC* is $\frac{(180° - 120°)}{2} = 30°$

So $x$ is 120° − 60° − 30° = 30°

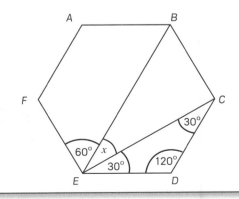

# Areas of Triangles and Quadrilaterals

## Area Calculations

### Area of a Triangle

If you know the length of the base and the **perpendicular** height, you can use the following formula to work out the area of a triangle:

**Area of triangle = $\frac{1}{2}$ × base × perpendicular height**

$$A = \frac{1}{2}bh$$

or

**Area of triangle = $\dfrac{\text{base} \times \text{perpendicular height}}{2}$**

$$A = \frac{bh}{2}$$

Perpendicular height, $h$

Base, $b$

If you know the length of two sides and the angle between them, you can use this formula to work out the area:

**Area of triangle = $\frac{1}{2}ab\sin C$**

*N.B. This formula is given on the formulae page of the examination paper.*

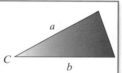

$a$

$C$    $b$

### Area of a Trapezium

**Area of trapezium = $\frac{1}{2}(a + b)h$**

*N.B. This formula is given on the formulae page of the examination paper.*

$a$

$h$

$b$

### Area of a Parallelogram

**Area of parallelogram = base × perpendicular height**

$$A = bh$$

$h$

$b$

---

### Example 1

Work out the area of these shapes:

**a)**

5.4 cm

6.2 cm

**Solution**

Area of triangle = $\dfrac{\text{base} \times \text{perpendicular height}}{2}$

$= \dfrac{6.2 \times 5.4}{2}$

$= 16.74\,\text{cm}^2$

**b)**

3.5 cm

4 cm

7.5 cm

**Solution**

Area of trapezium $= \frac{1}{2}(a + b)h$

$= \frac{1}{2}(3.5 + 7.5)4$

$= 22\,\text{cm}^2$

**c)**

6 cm

7 cm

8 cm

**Solution**

Area of parallelogram $=$ base × perpendicular height

$= 8 \times 6$ ◀ Don't mix up the perpendicular height with the sloping height

$= 48\,\text{cm}^2$

**d)**

5.2 cm

35°

4.3 cm

**Solution**

Area of triangle $= \frac{1}{2}ab\sin C$

$= \frac{1}{2} \times 5.2 \times 4.3 \times \sin 35°$

$= 6.4\,\text{cm}^2$ (to 1 d.p.)

---

**Key Words**     **Perpendicular • Trapezium • Parallelogram**

## Example 2

The total area of this shape is 37.31 cm².

Work out the perpendicular height of the triangle.

3.4 cm

8.2 cm

**Solution**

> **Problem Solving**
>
> You know the formula for the area of a triangle is $A = \frac{1}{2}bh$. You have all the information you need to find $A$ and $b$, so then you can rearrange the formula to calculate $h$.

Area of rectangle is $8.2 \times 3.4 = 27.88$ cm²

Area of triangle is $37.31 - 27.88 = 9.43$ cm²

$$\frac{\text{base} \times \text{perpendicular height}}{2} = 9.43$$

$$\frac{8.2 \times \text{perpendicular height}}{2} = 9.43$$

$$\text{Perpendicular height of triangle} = \frac{9.43 \times 2}{8.2}$$

$$= 2.3 \text{ cm}$$

## Example 3

The length of a rectangle is 3 cm more than its width. The area of the rectangle is 108 cm².

Work out the length of the rectangle.

**Solution**

> **Problem Solving**
>
> Set up an equation using the information given and solve it. Draw a sketch if it helps.

Let the width of the rectangle be $x$ cm.

So the length is $(x + 3)$ cm.

$x$ cm

$(x + 3)$ cm

Length × width = area of rectangle

So $x(x + 3) = 108$

$x^2 + 3x - 108 = 0$ ← Now you can see that there is a quadratic equation to solve

$(x + 12)(x - 9) = 0$

So $x + 12 = 0$ or $x - 9 = 0$

So $x = 9$ ← $x = -12$ is impossible as you can't have a negative width

Width of rectangle = 9 cm

and length of rectangle = 12 cm

## Quick Test

1 Work out the areas of these shapes. Give your answers to 2 decimal places.

a)

3.5 cm
4.6 cm

b)

4.2 cm
2.3 cm
6.8 cm

c)

3.6 cm
2.8 cm

d)

7.4 cm
49°
3.2 cm

# Circumference and Area of Circles

## Circle Facts

You need to know the following:

- The **circumference** of a circle is the distance around the edge of the circle.
- The **radius** of a circle is a straight line from the centre to the circumference.
- The **diameter** is a straight line through the centre joining opposite points on the circumference.

- A **chord** is a straight line joining any two points on the circumference.
- A **tangent** is a straight line that touches the circumference of a circle.
- An **arc** is a part of the circumference of a circle.
- A **sector** is the area enclosed by two radii and an arc.
- A **segment** is the area between a chord and its arc.

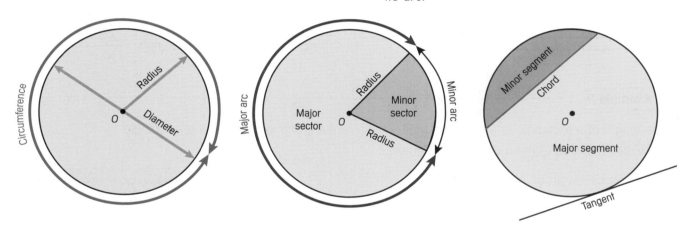

## Calculations with Circles

### Circumference of a Circle

**Circumference** is the word used to mean the **perimeter** of a circle.

The circumference of a circle is given by:

$$\textbf{Circumference} = \pi \times \textbf{diameter}$$
$$C = \pi d$$
or
$$\textbf{Circumference} = 2 \times \pi \times \textbf{radius}$$
$$C = 2\pi r$$

### Area of a Circle

The area of a circle is given by:

$$\textbf{Area} = \pi \times \textbf{radius}^2$$
$$A = \pi r^2$$

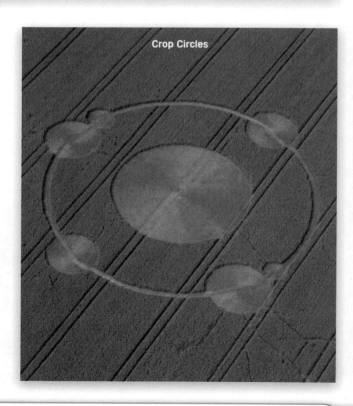

**Crop Circles**

**Key Words**  Circumference • Radius • Diameter • Chord • Tangent • Arc • Sector • Segment • Perimeter

# Circumference and Area of Circles

## Example 1

**a)** Work out the circumference of this circle. Give your answer to 2 decimal places.

5.4 cm

*O*

**Solution**

$C = 2\pi r$

$= 2 \times \pi \times 5.4$

$= 33.929...$

$= 33.93$ cm

> Remember to write down more than 2 decimal places before rounding

> You could get the same answer by working out the diameter (2 × 5.4 = 10.8 cm), then using the formula $C = \pi d$

**b)** Work out the area of the circle. Give your answer to 2 decimal places.

**Solution**

$A = \pi r^2 = \pi \times 5.4 \times 5.4$

$= 91.608...$

$= 91.61$ cm$^2$

## Example 2

**a)** Work out the circumference of this circle. Give your answer in terms of $\pi$.

8 cm

*O*

**Solution**

$C = 2\pi r = 2 \times \pi \times 8$

$= 16\pi$ cm

> Again, you could get the same answer by working out the diameter (2 × 8 = 16 cm), then using the formula $C = \pi d$. If you're asked to give an answer in terms of $\pi$, then leave the $\pi$ symbol in your answer

**b)** Work out the area of the circle. Give your answer in terms of $\pi$.

**Solution**

$A = \pi r^2 = \pi \times 8 \times 8$

$= 64\pi$ cm$^2$

## Example 3

Work out the perimeter of this semicircle. Give your answer to 2 decimal places.

6.7 cm

**Solution**

**Problem Solving**

When asked to work out the perimeter, remember to calculate all the lengths of the shape you are given (in this case the length of the circular arc of the semicircle plus the diameter).

Length of circular arc $= \frac{1}{2}(\pi \times 6.7) = 10.524...$

Perimeter is length of circular arc + diameter = 10.524... + 6.7

$= 17.22$ cm

## Quick Test

**1** Work out **i)** the circumference and **ii)** the area of these circles.
Give your answers to 1 decimal place.
**a)** A circle of radius 4.7 cm
**b)** A circle of diameter 6.1 cm
**c)** A circle of radius 2.4 cm

**2** Work out **i)** the circumference and **ii)** the area of these circles.
Give your answers in terms of $\pi$.
**a)** A circle of diameter 10 cm
**b)** A circle of radius 6 cm

# Arc Length and Area of a Sector

## Circumference and Area of a Circle

You need to remember the following:

> **Circumference of a circle = π × diameter**
>
> $$C = \pi d$$
>
> or
>
> **Circumference of a circle = 2 × π × radius**
>
> $$C = 2\pi r$$

> **Area of a circle = π × radius²**
>
> $$A = \pi r^2$$

## Arc Length and Area of a Sector

### Arc Length of a Circle

An **arc** is part of the circumference of a circle.
The length of an arc is given by:

> **Arc length** = $\dfrac{\text{angle at centre}}{360°}$ × $\begin{array}{c}\text{circumference}\\\text{of circle}\end{array}$

An arc that is:

- smaller than a semicircular arc is called a **minor arc**
- bigger than a semicircular arc is called a **major arc**.

### Area of a Sector of a Circle

A **sector** is the area enclosed by two radii and an arc. The area of a sector is given by:

> **Area of sector** = $\dfrac{\text{angle at centre}}{360°}$ × $\begin{array}{c}\text{area}\\\text{of circle}\end{array}$

A sector that is:

- smaller than a semicircle is called a **minor sector**
- bigger than a semicircle is called a **major sector**.

---

### Example 1

Work out the arc length and area of the sector shown. Give your answers to 1 decimal place.

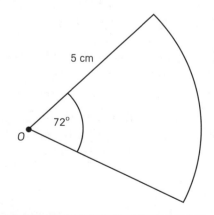

**Solution**

$$\text{Arc length} = \frac{\text{angle at centre}}{360°} \times \frac{\text{circumference}}{\text{of circle}}$$

$$= \frac{72°}{360°} \times 2 \times \pi \times 5$$

$$= 6.3 \text{ cm}$$

$$\text{Area of sector} = \frac{\text{angle at centre}}{360°} \times \text{area of circle}$$

$$= \frac{72°}{360°} \times \pi \times 5^2$$

$$= 15.7 \text{ cm}^2$$

## Example 2

The diagram shows a keyhole shape.

3 cm

60°

4 cm

**a)** Work out the perimeter of the shape. Give your answer to 1 decimal place.

**Solution**

> **Problem Solving**
>
> Break down the diagram into parts you can recognise (in this case an arc and three straight lines). Remember that the perimeter is just the length of the outside edge, i.e.

Triangle is equilateral so length of base = 7 cm

Angle at centre for major arc is $360° - 60° = 300°$

$$\text{Length of major arc} = \frac{\text{angle at centre}}{360°} \times \text{circumference of circle}$$

$$= \frac{300°}{360°} \times 2 \times \pi \times 3$$

$$= 15.70\ldots \text{ cm}$$

So the perimeter of the shape is:

$15.70\ldots + 4 + 4 + 7 = 30.7$ cm

**b)** Work out the area of the keyhole shape.

Give your answer to 1 decimal place.

**Solution**

> **Problem Solving**
>
> Break down the diagram into shapes you can recognise.

$$\text{Area of circle} = \pi \times 3^2$$

$$= 28.27\ldots \text{ cm}^2$$

$$\text{Area of triangle} = \frac{1}{2} \times 7 \times 7 \times \sin 60°$$

$$= 21.21\ldots \text{ cm}^2$$

$$\frac{\text{Area of}}{\text{minor sector}} = \frac{\text{angle at centre}}{360°} \times \frac{\text{area}}{\text{of circle}}$$

$$= \frac{60°}{360°} \times \pi \times 3^2$$

$$= 4.71\ldots \text{ cm}^2$$

Total area of the keyhole shape is given by:

$$\frac{\text{Area of}}{\text{circle}} + \frac{\text{area of}}{\text{triangle}} - \frac{\text{area of}}{\text{minor sector}}$$

$= 28.27\ldots + 21.21\ldots - 4.71\ldots$

$= 44.77\ldots$

$= 44.8$ cm$^2$

## Quick Test

1. Work out **i)** the arc length and **ii)** the area of these sectors. Give your answers to 1 decimal place.

   **a)**

   6 cm    115°

   **b)**

   9 cm
   42°

   **c)**

   190°
   4 cm

# Plan and Elevation

A **plan view** of a 3-D shape is what you see when you look at it from above.

The **front elevation** of a 3-D shape is what you see when you look at it from the front.

The **side elevation** of a 3-D shape is what you see when you look at it from the side.

---

**Example 1**

Here is a 3-D shape made of centimetre cubes drawn on isometric paper:

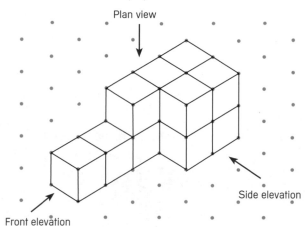

Plan view

Side elevation

Front elevation

Draw **a)** the plan view, **b)** the front elevation and **c)** the side elevation on squared paper.

**Solution**

**a)**

**b)**

**c)**

---

## Example 2

Here are the three views of a 3-D shape:

Plan view

Front elevation

Side elevation

Draw the 3-D shape on isometric paper.

**Solution**

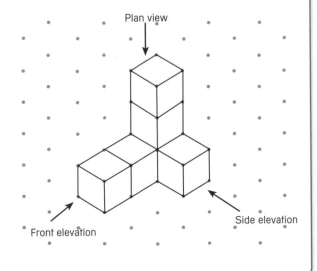

Plan view

Front elevation

Side elevation

## Quick Test

1 For each shape draw on squared paper:
   i) the plan view
   ii) the front elevation
   iii) the side elevation.

a)

b)

1 cm
2 cm
4 cm

c)

3 cm
1 cm
5 cm
3 cm
2 cm
1 cm

# Volumes of Prisms

## Volume Facts

You should know the following:

- **Volume** is the amount of space a 3-D shape fills.
- Common units for volume are $cm^3$ and $m^3$.

## Volume of a Cuboid

| **Volume of a cuboid = length × width × height** |
| :---: |
| $V = lwh$ |

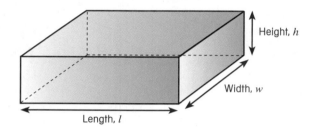

Height, $h$

Width, $w$

Length, $l$

---

**Example**

Work out the volume of this cuboid.

2 cm

4 cm

5 cm

**Solution**

Volume of cuboid = length × width × height

Volume = 5 × 4 × 2

= 40 $cm^3$

## Volume of a Prism

A **prism** is a 3-D shape that has **uniform cross-section**.

| **Volume of a prism = area of cross-section × length** |
| :---: |
| $V = Al$ |
| N.B. You're given this formula in the examination. |

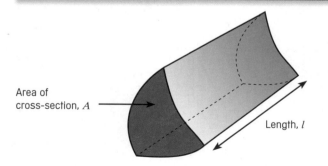

Area of cross-section, $A$

Length, $l$

---

**Example**

Work out the volume of this prism.

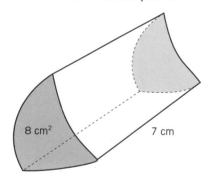

8 $cm^2$

7 cm

**Solution**

Volume of prism = area of cross-section × length

Volume = 8 × 7

= 56 $cm^3$

**Key Words**   Volume • Cuboid • Prism

## Volumes of Cylinders and Triangular Prisms

**Cylinders** and **triangular prisms** are special types of prism.

The cross-section of a cylinder is a circle, so:
- the area of the circle ($\pi r^2$) is the area of the cross-section
- the volume of a cylinder = area of circle × height ($V = \pi r^2 h$)

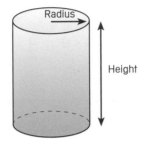

The cross-section of a triangular prism is a triangle, so:
- the area of the triangle ($\frac{1}{2}$ × base × height) is the area of the cross-section
- the volume of a triangular prism = area of triangle × length

## Quick Test

1. Work out the volume of these solids:
   a) A prism with cross-section 12 cm² and length 5 cm.
   b) A cylinder of height 4.2 cm and radius 6.1 cm.
   c) A triangular prism with base 4 cm, perpendicular height 3 cm and length 7 cm.

---

**Example 1**

Work out the volume of a cylinder of radius 4 cm and height 10 cm.

**Solution**

Volume of cylinder = $\pi \times 4^2 \times 10$ ← Area of circle × height

= $160\pi$ cm³ or 502.7 cm³

---

**Example 2**

Work out the volume of this triangular prism.

4 cm  6 cm  9 cm

**Solution**

Area of triangle = $\frac{1}{2} \times 6 \times 4$ ← $\frac{1}{2}$ × base × height

= 12 cm²

Volume of prism = 12 × 9 ← Area of cross-section × length

= 108 cm³

---

**Example 3**

You are given that 1 litre = 1000 cm³

A cylindrical water tank is $\frac{1}{4}$ full. How many more litres of water are needed to fill the tank?

15 cm  60 cm

**Solution**

| Problem Solving |
|---|
| Work out the volume of the whole shape, then work out the fraction you need. In this case you need $\frac{3}{4}$ of the total volume. |

Volume of full tank = $\pi \times 15 \times 15 \times 60$

= 42 412 cm³

Volume of $\frac{3}{4}$ of tank is $\frac{42\,412}{4} \times 3 = 31\,809$ cm³

So approximately 31.8 litres are needed to fill the tank.

---

**Key Words**     Cylinder • Triangular prism

# Volumes of Pyramids, Cones and Spheres

## Volume of a Pyramid

Volume of pyramid $= \frac{1}{3} \times$ **area of base × vertical height**

$$V = \frac{1}{3}Ah$$

### Example

Work out the volume of this pyramid.

9 cm

5 cm     4 cm

**Solution**

Volume of pyramid $= \frac{1}{3} \times$ area of base $\times$ vertical height

Volume $= \frac{1}{3} \times 5 \times 4 \times 9$

$= 60$ cm$^3$

## Volume of a Cone

A **cone** is a pyramid with a circular base.

Volume of a pyramid $= \frac{1}{3} \times$ area of base $\times$ vertical height

So:

**Volume of cone $= \frac{1}{3} \times \pi r^2 \times h$**

$$V = \frac{1}{3}\pi r^2 h$$

N.B. You're given this formula in the examination.

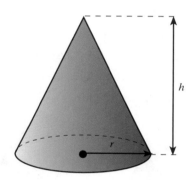

$h$

$r$

### Example

Work out the volume of this cone.

5 cm

3 cm

**Solution**

Volume of cone $= \frac{1}{3}\pi r^2 h$

Volume $= \frac{1}{3} \times \pi \times 3 \times 3 \times 5$

$= 15\pi$ cm$^3$ or 47.1 cm$^3$

## Volume of a Sphere

**Volume of sphere $= \frac{4}{3}\pi r^3$**

N.B. You're given this formula in the examination.

$r$

**Pyramid • Cone • Sphere**

# Volumes of Pyramids, Cones and Spheres

## Example

Work out the volume of this sphere.

6 cm

**Solution**

Volume of sphere $= \frac{4}{3}\pi r^3$

$\qquad$ Volume $= \frac{4}{3} \times \pi \times 6^3$

$\qquad\qquad = 288\pi$ cm$^3$ or 904.8 cm$^3$

## Hemispheres and Frustums

A **hemisphere** is half a sphere.

**Volume of hemisphere $= \frac{2}{3}\pi r^3$**

A **frustum** is the remainder of a regular solid whose upper part has been cut off by a plane parallel to the base.

Pyramid

Pyramid

Frustum

Cone

Cone

Frustum

## Example

A frustum is made from pyramid A by removing pyramid B. The base of pyramid A is a square of side 8 cm and the height is 12 cm. The base of pyramid B is a square of side 3 cm and the height is 4.5 cm. Work out the volume of the frustum.

Pyramid A

Pyramid B

Frustum

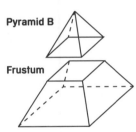

**Solution**

| Problem Solving |
|---|
| Work out the volume of each pyramid. Subtract the volume of the smaller pyramid from the volume of the larger one. |

Volume of pyramid A $= \frac{1}{3} \times 8 \times 8 \times 12$

$\qquad\qquad = 256$ cm$^3$

Volume of pyramid B $= \frac{1}{3} \times 3 \times 3 \times 4.5$

$\qquad\qquad = 13.5$ cm$^3$

So volume of frustum is $256 - 13.5$

$\qquad\qquad = 242.5$ cm$^3$

## Quick Test

1. Work out the volume of these solids. Give your answers to 1 decimal place.
   a) A hemisphere of radius 2.3 cm.
   b) A cone with base radius 3.5 cm and height 5 cm.
   c) A square-based pyramid of base length 4 cm and vertical height 6.5 cm.

# Pythagoras' Theorem

## The Hypotenuse

The **hypotenuse** is:

- the **longest side** on a **right-angled triangle**
- opposite the right angle.

## Pythagoras' Theorem

**Pythagoras' theorem** states that the square on the hypotenuse is equal to the sum of the squares on the other two sides. So, $c^2 = a^2 + b^2$

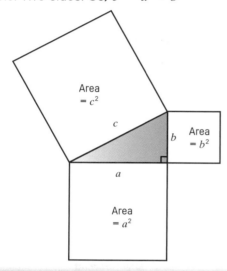

Area = $c^2$

$c$

$b$ Area = $b^2$

$a$

Area = $a^2$

**Example**

Work out the length of the hypotenuse in this right-angled triangle.

5 cm

12 cm

**Solution**

Pythagoras' theorem states that $c^2 = a^2 + b^2$

So $c^2$ is $12^2 + 5^2 = 144 + 25$

$c^2 = 169$

So $c$ is $\sqrt{169} = 13$ cm

## Pythagorean Triples

A **Pythagorean triple** is where the values of $a$, $b$ and $c$ are all whole numbers, e.g. (3, 4, 5), (6, 8, 10), (5, 12, 13), (7, 24, 25) and (8, 15, 17).

**Example**

Work out the area of this isosceles triangle.

10 cm

$h$

16 cm

**Problem Solving**

An isosceles triangle can be broken up into two right-angled triangles, so you can use Pythagoras' theorem to work out the height. You then have all the information you need to work out the area.

**Solution**

So $10^2 = h^2 + 8^2$

$100 = h^2 + 64$

$100 - 64 = h^2$

$36 = h^2$

So $h = 6$ cm ←

$h$   10 cm

8 cm

You may have spotted this is a Pythagorean triple. If so, you can just state the height is 6 cm because it's a 6, 8, 10 Pythagorean triple

Area = $\frac{1}{2} \times 16 \times 6$ ←   $\frac{1}{2} \times$ base × height

Area = 48 cm²

## Pythagoras' Theorem in 3-D

3-D problems can be broken down into smaller 2-D problems. You should always try to draw diagrams showing right-angled triangles in 2-D because this will make the problem easier.

### Example

Work out the length of the diagonal in this cuboid.

### Solution

**Problem Solving**

You will have to work with other triangles within the shape to obtain the answer.

There are several right-angled triangles in this cuboid.

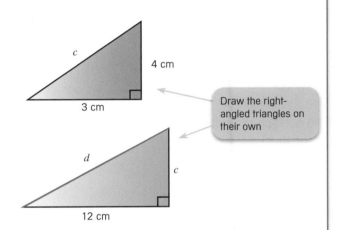

Draw the right-angled triangles on their own

Using the first triangle, this is a Pythagorean triple (3, 4, 5), so $c$ = 5 cm

Using the second triangle, this is also a Pythagorean triple (5, 12, 13), so $d$ = 13 cm

So the diagonal is 13 cm.

## Quick Test

1. Work out the length of the missing sides in these right-angled triangles:

a)

15 cm

8 cm

b)

9 cm

4 cm

c)

5 cm

8 cm

# Surface Area

## Surface Area and Nets

The **surface area** of a solid:
- is the total area of all the surfaces added together
- is equal to the area of the **net** of the shape.

### Cube

The surface area of a cube is the total area of the six squares.

### Cuboid

The surface area of a cuboid is the total area of the six faces.

### Triangular Prism

The surface area of a triangular prism is the total area of the two triangles and the three rectangles.

### Cylinder

The surface area of a cylinder is the total of the area of the two circles on each end and the **curved surface area**.

The curved surface opens out to form a rectangle with length equal to the circumference of the circular end.

| Curved surface area | = | circumference of end | × | height of cylinder |
|---|---|---|---|---|

$$C = 2\pi r \times h$$

$$C = 2\pi rh$$

Area of one end $= \pi r^2$

Total surface area $= 2\pi rh + 2\pi r^2$

Circumference

Height

## Cone

The total surface area of a cone is the total of the area of the circular base and the curved surface area.

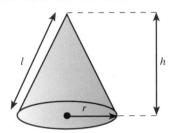

| Curved surface area of cone | $= \pi \times$ radius $\times$ slant height |

$$C = \pi r l$$

**Total surface area** $= \pi r l + \pi r^2$

*N.B. You're given the formula for the curved surface area of a cone in the examination.*

## Sphere

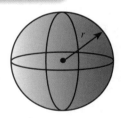

| Curved surface area of sphere | $= 4 \times \pi \times$ radius$^2$ |

$$C = 4\pi r^2$$

*N.B. You're given the formula for the curved surface area of a sphere in the examination.*

## Quick Test

1. Work out the total surface area of these shapes:
   a) A cube with edge 3 cm.
   b) A cuboid with edges 5 cm, 3 cm and 2 cm.
   c) A triangular prism with a right-angled triangle cross-section and with base 4 cm, height 3 cm and length 10 cm.
   d) A cylinder with radius 3 cm and height 12 cm. Leave your answer in terms of $\pi$.
   e) A cone with radius 3 cm, height 4 cm and slant height 5 cm.

### Example 1

Work out the total surface area of this cylinder. Give your answer to 1 decimal place.

**Solution**

Area of one end $= \pi r^2$

$= \pi \times 4^2$

$= 50.26\ldots$ cm$^2$

Curved surface area $= 2\pi r h$

$= 2 \times \pi \times 4 \times 9$

$= 226.19\ldots$ cm$^2$

Total surface area $= 2\pi r h + 2\pi r^2$

$= 226.19\ldots + 50.26\ldots + 50.26\ldots$

$= 326.7$ cm$^2$

### Example 2

Work out the total surface area of this cone. Give your answer to 1 decimal place.

**Solution**

**Problem Solving**

You're not given the slant height but the sloping side forms a right-angled triangle with the radius and vertical height. This means you can work out the slant height using Pythagorean triples.

Area of base $= \pi r^2$

$= \pi \times 5^2$

$= 78.53\ldots$ cm$^2$

Curved surface area $= \pi r l$

$= \pi \times 5 \times 13$    Slant height is 13 cm (5, 12, 13 Pythagorean triple)

$= 204.20\ldots$ cm$^2$

Total surface area $= \pi r l + \pi r^2$

$= 204.20\ldots + 78.53\ldots$

$= 282.7$ cm$^2$

# Trigonometry in Right-angled Triangles

## Labelling Sides and Trigonometrical Ratios

Trigonometry is used to work out unknown lengths or unknown angles in **right-angled triangles**:

- The **hypotenuse** is opposite the right angle.
- The **opposite side** is opposite the marked angle ($x$).
- The **adjacent side** is next to the marked angle ($x$).

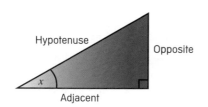

The three trigonometrical ratios you will use are called **sine**, **cosine** and **tangent**. In a right-angled triangle:

| | | S | O | H |
|---|---|---|---|---|
| $\sin x = \dfrac{\text{opposite}}{\text{hypotenuse}}$ | | **S**ix | **O**ld | **H**orses |
| $\cos x = \dfrac{\text{adjacent}}{\text{hypotenuse}}$ | | **C**lumsy | **A**nd | **H**eavy |
| $\tan x = \dfrac{\text{opposite}}{\text{adjacent}}$ | | **T**rod | **O**n | **A**lbert |

*N.B. You have to remember these for the examination.*

## Working out a Length and Working out an Angle

To **work out a length** using trigonometry:
1. Label the sides (hyp, opp, adj) in this order.
2. Circle the given side and the one you want to work out.
3. Choose the correct ratio.
4. Set up and solve the equation.

### Example

Work out the length $x$.

**Solution**

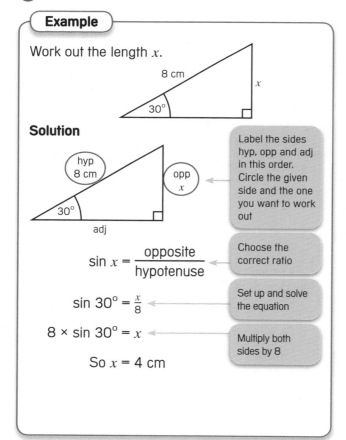

Label the sides hyp, opp and adj in this order. Circle the given side and the one you want to work out

$$\sin x = \frac{\text{opposite}}{\text{hypotenuse}}$$

Choose the correct ratio

$$\sin 30° = \frac{x}{8}$$

Set up and solve the equation

$$8 \times \sin 30° = x$$

Multiply both sides by 8

$$\text{So } x = 4 \text{ cm}$$

To **work out an angle** using trigonometry:
1. Label the sides (hyp, opp, adj) in this order.
2. Circle the two given sides.
3. Choose the correct ratio.
4. Set up and solve the equation.

### Example

Work out the size of angle $x$.

**Solution**

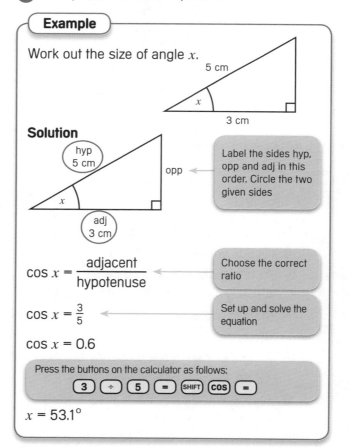

Label the sides hyp, opp and adj in this order. Circle the two given sides

$$\cos x = \frac{\text{adjacent}}{\text{hypotenuse}}$$

Choose the correct ratio

$$\cos x = \frac{3}{5}$$

Set up and solve the equation

$$\cos x = 0.6$$

Press the buttons on the calculator as follows:

3 ÷ 5 = SHIFT COS =

$$x = 53.1°$$

**Trigonometry • Hypotenuse • Opposite side • Adjacent side • Sine • Cosine**

# Trigonometry in Right-angled Triangles

## Angles of Elevation and Depression

An **angle of elevation** is the angle measured above a horizontal direction.

An **angle of depression** is the angle measured below a horizontal direction.

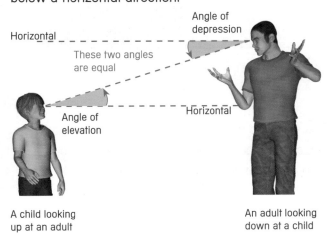

A child looking up at an adult

An adult looking down at a child

A builder stands 5 metres from a building. He is 1.8 metres tall.

Work out the height of the building.

**Solution**

> **Problem Solving**
>
> Work out the height in the same way that you would find an unknown length in any right-angled triangle but remember to add on the height of the builder.

$$\tan x = \frac{\text{opposite}}{\text{adjacent}}$$

> Use $x$ for the height of the triangle

$$\tan 40° = \frac{x}{5}$$

$$5 \times \tan 40° = x$$

> Multiply both sides by 5

$$\text{So } x = 4.2 \text{ m (1 d.p.)}$$

So height of building is 4.2 + 1.8 = 6 metres

## Trigonometry in 3-D

3-D problems can be broken down to make smaller 2-D problems. You should always try to draw diagrams showing right-angled triangles in 2-D as this will make the problem easier.

### Quick Test

1. Work out the value of $x$ in each diagram.

**Example**

The diagram shows a square-based pyramid. The sides of the square are 6 cm. The sloping edges are 5 cm.

Work out the angle *VMX* (marked $x$).

**Solution**

> Draw the right-angled triangles on their own

Triangle *VBM* is a Pythagorean triple, so *VM* is 4 cm.

Looking at triangle *VMX* gives $\cos x = \frac{3}{4}$

So $x = 41.4°$

---

**Key Words**     Tangent • Angle of elevation • Angle of depression

# Sine and Cosine Rules

## Working out Unknown Lengths and Angles in Triangles

The **sine rule** and **cosine rule** can be used in a triangle to work out:

- an unknown length
- an unknown angle.

If a triangle has vertices $A$, $B$ and $C$, then the sides opposite each angle are $a$, $b$ and $c$ respectively.

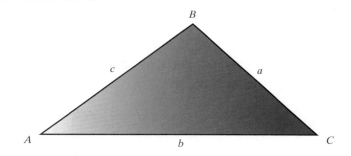

## Sine Rule

This is the sine rule:

$$\frac{a}{\sin A} = \frac{b}{\sin B} = \frac{c}{\sin C}$$

N.B. You're given this in the examination.

The equation can also be used 'upside down', i.e.

$$\frac{\sin A}{a} = \frac{\sin B}{b} = \frac{\sin C}{c}$$

The sine rule can be used when you know both values for a particular letter (e.g. $A$ and $a$) together with one other value. So you could use the sine rule if you knew $A$, $a$ and $b$ or $A$, $a$ and $C$.

To use the sine rule:

1. label the sides
2. write out the formula
3. circle the parts you know
4. set up and solve the equation.

### Example 1

Work out the length of $AC$ in this triangle.

**Solution**

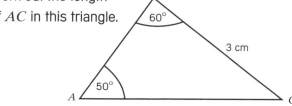

$$\frac{\textcircled{a}}{\textcircled{\sin A}} = \frac{b}{\textcircled{\sin B}} = \frac{c}{\sin C}$$

Label the sides. In this triangle $a$ = 3 cm, $A = 50°$, $B = 60°$

Write out the formula and circle the known parts
$\frac{c}{\sin C}$ isn't used here

So $\frac{3}{\sin 50°} = \frac{b}{\sin 60°}$

Set up the equation

$\frac{3 \times \sin 60°}{\sin 50°} = b$

Multiply both sides by sin 60°

So $b$ (side $AC$) = 3.4 cm

### Example 2

Work out the size of angle $B$ in this triangle.

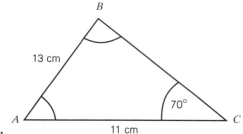

**Solution**

Label the sides, then write out the formula and circle the known parts. Then identify which part of the formula isn't needed

So $\frac{11}{\sin B} = \frac{13}{\sin 70°}$

Set up the equation

$11 \times \sin 70° = 13 \times \sin B$

Multiply both sides by sin $B$ and sin 70°

$\frac{11 \times \sin 70°}{13} = \sin B$

So $\sin B = 0.795...$

Divide both sides by 13

$B = 52.7°$

Sine rule • Cosine rule

## Cosine Rule

This is the cosine rule:

$$a^2 = b^2 + c^2 - 2bc \cos A$$

N.B. You're given this in the examination.

This can be rearranged to:

$$\cos A = \frac{b^2 + c^2 - a^2}{2bc}$$

N.B. You're **not** given this in the examination.

The cosine rule can be used when you know two sides and the angle between them, e.g. $b$, $c$ and $A$, or when you know all three sides, i.e. $a$, $b$ and $c$.

To use the cosine rule:

**1** label the sides

**2** write out the formula

**3** circle the parts you know

**4** set up and solve the equation.

N.B. It's easier to use the labels $b$, $c$ and $A$ to match the formula given.

---

### Example 1

Work out the length of $BC$ in this triangle.

**Solution**

> Label the sides. In this triangle $b = 6$ cm, $c = 8$ cm, $A = 34°$

$$a^2 = b^2 + c^2 - 2bc \cos A$$

> Write out the formula

So $a^2 = 6^2 + 8^2 - (2 \times 6 \times 8 \cos 34°)$

> Set up the equation

$a^2 = 20.4...$

> $a$ = the square root of 20.4...

So $a$ (side $BC$) = 4.52 cm

---

## Quick Test

**1** Work out $x$ in each part.

**a)**

**b)**

**c)**

**d)**

---

### Example 2

Look at the triangle.

**a)** Work out the size of angle $A$.

**Solution**

> Label the sides. In this triangle $a = 7$ cm, $b = 8$ cm, $c = 6$ cm

$$\cos A = \frac{b^2 + c^2 - a^2}{2bc}$$

> Use the rearranged formula when given three sides

$$\cos A = \frac{8^2 + 6^2 - 7^2}{2 \times 8 \times 6}$$

$\cos A = 0.53125$, so $A = 57.9°$

**b)** Which angle is the biggest? Give a reason for your answer.

**Solution**

**Problem Solving**

In any triangle, the biggest angle is always opposite the longest side and the smallest angle is always opposite the shortest side.

Angle $B$ is biggest because $b$ (side $AC$) is the longest side.

# Circle Theorems

## Tangents

A **tangent** is a straight line that touches the circle at a point on the circumference. Here are some properties relating to tangents of circles:

- The angle between a tangent and the radius at the point on the circumference is 90°.
- Tangents to a circle drawn from the same point are equal in length.
- The triangles formed using tangents from a common point, radii and a line drawn from the centre are **congruent** right-angled triangles.

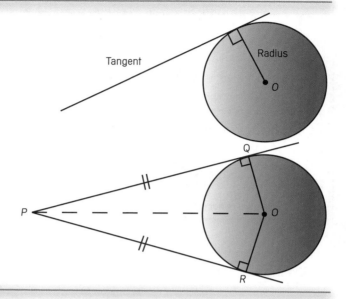

## Chords

A radius drawn **perpendicular** (at 90°) to a chord bisects the chord.

Triangle *OXZ* is isosceles

## Circle Theorems

### Basic Circle Theorems

You need to know these basic circle theorems:

| This diagram shows an angle $x$ **subtended** by an arc. | The angle at the centre of a circle is twice the angle at the circumference that is subtended by the same arc. | Any angle at the circumference that is subtended by a diameter is 90°. | Angles at the circumference, in the same segment and subtended by the same arc, are equal. |
|---|---|---|---|
|  |  |  |  |

**Key Words**     **Tangent • Congruent • Perpendicular • Subtend**

## Cyclic Quadrilaterals

A **cyclic quadrilateral** is a quadrilateral with all four vertices on the circumference of a circle.

Opposite angles of a cyclic quadrilateral add up to 180°.

$x + y = 180°$

$a + b = 180°$

## Alternate Segment Theorem

The angle between a tangent and a chord through the point of contact is equal to the angle at the circumference in the **alternate segment**, subtended by the chord.

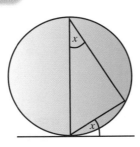

### Quick Test

1. Work out the value of the lettered angle in each part.

a)

b)

c)

d)

---

### Example 1

Work out the size of $x$.

**Solution**
The angle at the centre is twice the angle at the circumference.

So $x$ is $\dfrac{106°}{2} = 53°$

### Example 2

Work out the size of $y$.

**Solution**
Angle at circumference = 90°

So $y$ is $180° - 90° - 23° = 67°$

### Example 3

Work out the size of $z$.

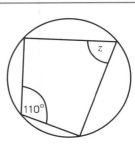

**Solution**
Opposite angles of a cyclic quadrilateral add up to 180°.

So $z$ is $180° - 110° = 70°$

### Example 4

Work out the size of $x$ and the size of $y$.

**Solution**
$x = 77°$ ⟵ Alternate segment theorem

So $y$ is $180° - 62° - 77° = 41°$

---

# Transformations

## Types of Transformation

A **transformation** changes the appearance of a shape. It may change the shape's **position**, **size** or **orientation**.

You'll need to draw or describe **reflections**, **rotations**, **translations** and **enlargements** of 2-D shapes. The original shape is called the **object**. The transformed shape is called the **image**.

### Reflections

A **reflection** transforms a shape so that it's a **mirror image** of the original shape. The object and the image have line symmetry.

To describe a reflection you have to state the position of the mirror line, e.g. a reflection in the $x$-axis or a reflection in the line $x = 2$

Each point on the object is the same distance from the mirror line as its corresponding point on the image

### Rotations

A **rotation** transforms a shape so that the original shape is **turned about** a fixed point. The fixed point is called the **centre of rotation**.

To describe a rotation you have to state:
- the angle turned with the direction of turn (clockwise or anticlockwise)
- the centre of rotation.

For example, a rotation 90° clockwise about (0, 0) or a rotation 180° about (3, 2).

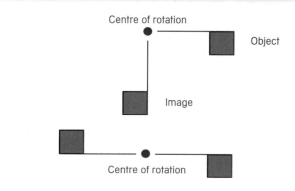

Each point on the object is the same distance from the centre of rotation as its corresponding point on the image

### Translations

A **translation** transforms a shape so that the original shape **moves** without reflecting or rotating.

To describe a translation you have to state:
- the distance moved horizontally
- the distance moved vertically.

This can be written in words, e.g. 3 units to the right and 2 units down, or 4 units to the left and 5 units up.

Translations can also be written as **vectors**, e.g. $\binom{3}{-2}$ and $\binom{-4}{5}$:
- The top number is the horizontal movement (right is positive and left is negative).
- The bottom number is the vertical movement (up is positive and down is negative).

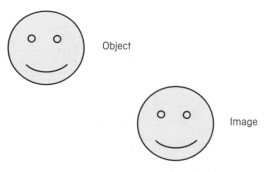

Every point in the shape moves in the same direction and through the same distance

**Key Words**     Transformation • Reflection • Rotation • Translation • Enlargement • Vector

## Enlargements

An **enlargement** transforms a shape so that the original shape **increases** or **decreases** in size. The **scale factor** of an enlargement shows how the lengths of a shape increase or decrease, e.g. for a scale factor 2, the lengths double.

To describe an enlargement you have to state:
- the centre of enlargement
- the scale factor of the enlargement.

For example, an enlargement, centre (0, 0), scale factor 2.

A **fractional scale factor** means the image will be **smaller** than the object.

A **negative scale factor** means the image will be on the **opposite side** of the centre of enlargement to the original shape.

### Example 1

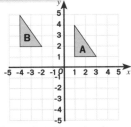

a) Describe the single transformation that takes triangle A to triangle B.

**Solution**
Translation 5 units to the left and 1 unit up or translation $\binom{-5}{1}$

b) Reflect triangle A in the line $y = -x$. Label it C.

**Solution**

### Example 2

Enlarge triangle A with scale factor 2 and centre of enlargement (0, 1). Label it B.

**Solution**
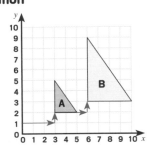

### Example 3

Triangle A is translated $\binom{-5}{0}$ to form triangle B. Triangle B is then rotated 180° about the origin to form triangle C. Describe the single transformation that takes triangle A to triangle C.

**Solution**

Triangle A to triangle C is a rotation of 180° about (2.5, 0).

## Quick Test

1. Describe the single transformation that takes:
   a) triangle A to triangle B
   b) triangle A to triangle C
   c) triangle A to triangle D.

# Congruency and Similarity

## Congruent Shapes

Two shapes are **congruent** if they're the **same size** and the **same shape**.

When shapes are reflected, rotated or translated, the image is congruent to the object.

All these shapes are congruent:

## Congruent Triangles

Corresponding sides in two triangles are sides in the same position or opposite the same angle.

Two triangles are congruent if they satisfy any one of the following four conditions:

| Side, Side, Side (SSS) | Side, Angle, Side (SAS) | Angle, Angle, Corresponding Side (AA corr S) | Right angle, Hypotenuse, Side (RHS) |
|---|---|---|---|
| All three sides of one triangle are equal to the three sides in the other triangle. | Two sides and the included angle of one triangle are equal to the two sides and the included angle in the other triangle. | Two angles and a corresponding side of one triangle are equal to two angles and a corresponding side of the other triangle. | Both triangles have a right angle, an equal hypotenuse and another equal side. |
| <br> | <br> | <br> | 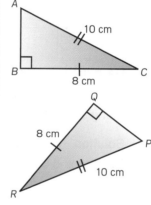 |
| $AB = PQ$, $BC = QR$, $AC = PR$, so congruent (SSS). | $AB = PQ$, $AC = PR$, angle $A$ = angle $P$, so congruent (SAS). | Angle $A$ = angle $P$, angle $B$ = angle $Q$, $BC = QR$, so congruent (AA corr S). | Angle $B$ = angle $Q$, $AC = PR$, $BC = QR$, so congruent (RHS). |

## Example

Prove that triangles *ABC* and *PQR* are congruent.

**Solution**

### Problem Solving

Look at the information you are given – these are right-angled triangles with one equal side. You can use Pythagoras' theorem to find the hypotenuse of triangle *ABC* and see if they match to satisfy RHS.

Using Pythagorean triples in triangle *ABC*, $AC = 5$ cm

Angle $B$ = Angle $Q$ = $90°$ (right angle)

$AC = PR = 5$ cm (hypotenuse)

$AB = PQ = 4$ cm (side)

So the triangles are congruent (RHS).

## Similar Shapes

Two shapes are **similar** if one shape is an enlargement of the other:

- The angles in one shape will be equal to the corresponding angles in the other shape.
- The corresponding sides of each shape are in the same ratio.

The angles in both triangles are 50°, 60° and 70° so the triangles are similar.

The lengths on triangle $ABC$ are twice the corresponding lengths on triangle $PQR$ as 9.2 cm = 2 × 4.6 cm

So $\frac{AB}{PQ} = \frac{BC}{QR} = \frac{AC}{PR}$

$\frac{9.2}{4.6} = \frac{8.4}{QR} = \frac{AC}{5}$

$2 = \frac{8.4}{QR}$ and $2 = \frac{AC}{5}$

So $QR = 4.2$ cm and $AC = 10$ cm

### Example 1

Triangles $ABC$ and $PQR$ are similar. Work out the length of $PR$.

**Solution A**

$\frac{AB}{PQ} = \frac{AC}{PR}$

$\frac{5}{7.5} = \frac{8}{PR}$

$PR = \frac{8 \times 7.5}{5}$ ← Rearranging

$PR = 12$ cm

**Solution B**

$PQ$ is 1.5 times $AB$.
So $PR$ is $AC \times 1.5$
$= 12$ cm

### Areas and Volumes

When 2-D or 3-D shapes are similar and their corresponding lengths are in the ratio $x : y$

- **Area ratio** = $x^2 : y^2$
- **Volume ratio** = $x^3 : y^3$

### Example 2

Cuboid A is similar to cuboid B.

Write down the ratio of their surface areas and the ratio of their volumes.

**Solution**

The ratio of length is $8 : 4 = 2 : 1$

So the ratio of the surface areas is $2^2 : 1^2 = 4 : 1$

The ratio of volumes is $2^3 : 1^3 = 8 : 1$

## Quick Test

1. Why are these triangles congruent?

2. In the diagram $BC$ is parallel to $DE$.

Work out the length of $CE$.

3. The radii of two spheres are 6 cm and 9 cm.
   Write down the ratio of their volumes in its simplest form.

# Vectors

## Vectors

A **vector** is a quantity that has both **magnitude** (size) and **direction**. Examples of vectors are velocity and force.

Vectors are usually represented by a line with an arrow on it. The vector may be labelled:
- at each end with capital letters
- with a small letter (printed in bold type but handwritten as <u>a</u>).

For example, here $\overrightarrow{AB}$ = **a**

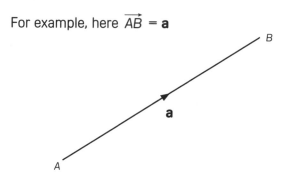

## Adding and Subtracting Vectors

To add two vectors, you can draw them so that they join up. So if **a** represents the vector $\binom{4}{3}$ and **b** represents the vector $\binom{3}{-1}$, the **resultant a + b** is:

$$\binom{4}{3} + \binom{3}{-1} = \binom{7}{2}$$

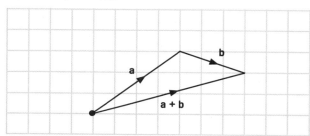

To subtract a vector is to reverse the direction, so
**a − b** is $\binom{4}{3} - \binom{3}{-1} = \binom{1}{4}$

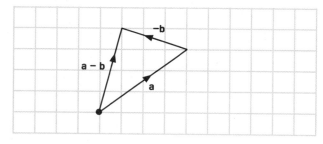

We can also write $\overrightarrow{AB} + \overrightarrow{BC} = \overrightarrow{AC}$ because translating from A to B and then B to C is equivalent to A to C.

### Example

A is the point $(1, 2)$. $\overrightarrow{AB} = \binom{5}{-3}$. Work out the coordinates of B.

**Solution**

**Problem Solving**

Use a grid to work out the solution to this type of question.

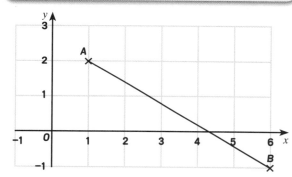

The coordinates of B are $(6, -1)$

**Key Words**

**Vector • Magnitude • Direction**

## Multiples of Vectors

A vector that is a multiple of another vector is:

- in the same direction (parallel or in the same line)
- bigger (or smaller) by the same factor as the multiple.

For example if $\overrightarrow{AB}$ = **a** + 4**b** and $\overrightarrow{CD}$ = 2**a** + 8**b**, then $\overrightarrow{CD}$ = 2 × $\overrightarrow{AB}$. This means:

- $\overrightarrow{CD}$ is in the same direction as $\overrightarrow{AB}$
- $\overrightarrow{CD}$ is twice the size of $\overrightarrow{AB}$.

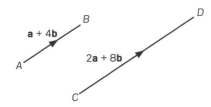

If $\overrightarrow{PQ}$ = 2**a** − 3**b** and $\overrightarrow{PR}$ = 6**a** − 9**b**, then $\overrightarrow{PR}$ = 3 × $\overrightarrow{PQ}$. This means:

- $\overrightarrow{PR}$ is three times the size of $\overrightarrow{PQ}$
- as $\overrightarrow{PQ}$ and $\overrightarrow{PR}$ both pass through $P$ in the same direction, $P$, $Q$ and $R$ are in the same straight line. This is called **collinear**.

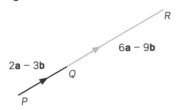

### Quick Test

1. $\overrightarrow{OA}$ = **a**, $\overrightarrow{OB}$ = **b**, $\overrightarrow{OC}$ = 2**a** − 3**b**
   Work out the following vectors.
   a) $\overrightarrow{BA}$
   b) $\overrightarrow{AC}$
   c) $\overrightarrow{CB}$

2. Work out:
   a) $\begin{pmatrix} 5 \\ -2 \end{pmatrix} + \begin{pmatrix} -3 \\ 4 \end{pmatrix}$
   b) $\begin{pmatrix} 1 \\ 0 \end{pmatrix} - \begin{pmatrix} 2 \\ -4 \end{pmatrix}$

### Example

In triangle $OAB$, $\overrightarrow{OA}$ = **a**, $\overrightarrow{OB}$ = **b**. The point $X$ divides the line $AB$ in the ratio 2 : 1

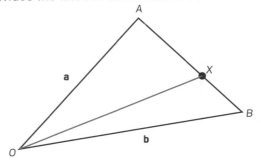

a) Work out the vector $\overrightarrow{AB}$ in terms of **a** and **b**.

**Solution**
$\overrightarrow{AB}$ = $\overrightarrow{AO}$ + $\overrightarrow{OB}$
$\overrightarrow{AB}$ = −**a** + **b**

b) Work out the vector $\overrightarrow{OX}$ in terms of **a** and **b**.

**Solution**
$\overrightarrow{AX}$ = $\frac{2}{3}\overrightarrow{AB}$

$\overrightarrow{AX}$ = $-\frac{2}{3}$**a** + $\frac{2}{3}$**b**

$\overrightarrow{OX}$ = $\overrightarrow{OA}$ + $\overrightarrow{AX}$

$\overrightarrow{OX}$ = **a** $- \frac{2}{3}$**a** + $\frac{2}{3}$**b**

$\overrightarrow{OX}$ = $\frac{1}{3}$**a** + $\frac{2}{3}$**b**

c) $\overrightarrow{OC}$ = **a** + 2**b**. What can you say about the points $O$, $X$ and $C$?

**Solution**
$\overrightarrow{OC}$ = **a** + 2**b**

So $\overrightarrow{OC}$ = 3$\overrightarrow{OX}$

> Remember that if a vector is a multiple of another vector, they are in the same direction

So $O$, $C$ and $X$ are collinear and $X$ divides $OC$ in the ratio 1 : 2

# Conversions, Bearings and Scale Drawings

## Conversions

For the examination you need to learn these **conversions** from **metric** to **imperial** measurements:

- 1 kg ≈ 2.2 pounds
- 1 litre ≈ $1\frac{3}{4}$ pints
- 4.5 litres ≈ 1 gallon
- 8 km ≈ 5 miles
- 30 cm ≈ 1 foot

You should also know common metric conversions:

| Length | 1 m = 100 cm |
| | 1 km = 1000 m |
| | 1 m = 1000 mm |
| | 1 cm = 10 mm |
| Mass | 1 tonne = 1000 kg |
| | 1 kg = 1000 g |

### Example 1

Convert 56 km to miles.

**Solution**

8 km ≈ 5 miles

So 1 km ≈ $\frac{5}{8}$ mile ← Divide by 8

56 km is $\frac{5}{8}$ × 56 = 35 miles ← Multiply by 56

### Example 2

Use the graph to convert:

**a)** 16 gallons into litres

**b)** 40 litres to gallons.

**Solution**

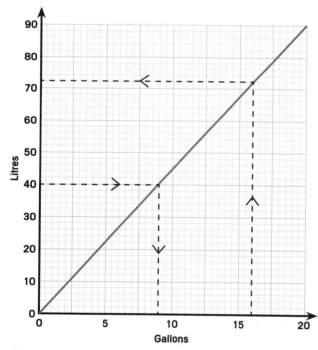

**a)** 16 gallons ≈ 72 litres

**b)** 40 litres ≈ 9 gallons

## Bearings and Scale Drawings

A **bearing** gives the direction to one place from another.

To measure a **three-figure bearing**:
- start from North
- measure clockwise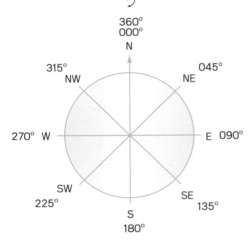

Three-figure bearings should always be given using three digits, e.g. a bearing of 45° is written 045°.

The diagram shows a map drawn to scale showing two towns, A and B.

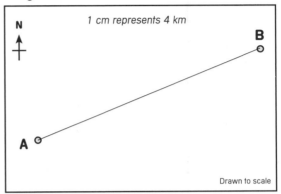

1 cm represents 4 km

Drawn to scale

**a)** Work out the bearing and the actual distance from A to B.

**Solution**

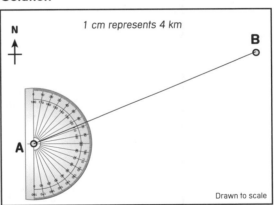

1 cm represents 4 km

Drawn to scale

Bearing is 067°
AB on the map is 6.4 cm, so the actual distance is 6.4 × 4 = 25.6 km

**b)** Work out the bearing of A from B.

**Solution**
067° + 180° = 247°

If two bearings are in opposite directions, the difference between the bearings is 180°

## Quick Test

1 Sketch bearings of:
   **a)** 030°   **b)** 140°   **c)** 270°

# Constructions

## Accurate Drawings

A **construction** is an accurate drawing using a combination of ruler, protractor and a pair of compasses. In your examination it's important that

when you use a pair of compasses, the construction arcs are clearly shown and that all lengths and angles are accurate.

---

### Example 1

**a)** Construct triangle ABC with AB = 3 cm, BC = 2.5 cm and AC = 2 cm

**Solution**

Draw AB of length 3 cm and draw arc from A of radius 2 cm

Draw arc from B of radius 2.5 cm and complete the triangle

**b)** Construct triangle ABC with AB = 3 cm, AC = 2 cm and angle BAC = 70°

**Solution**

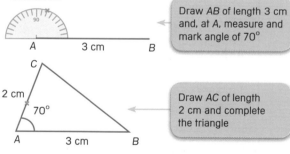

Draw AB of length 3 cm and, at A, measure and mark angle of 70°

Draw AC of length 2 cm and complete the triangle

**c)** Construct triangle ABC with AB = 2 cm, AC = 2 cm and angle ABC = 50°

**Solution**

Draw AB of length 2 cm and, at B, measure, mark and draw angle of 50°

Draw arc from A of radius 2 cm and complete the triangle

---

### Example 2

**a)** Use a ruler and a pair of compasses only to construct an angle of 60°.

**Solution**

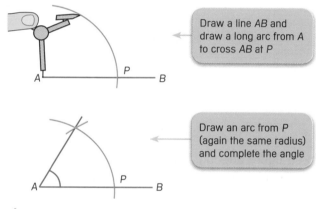

Draw a line AB and draw a long arc from A to cross AB at P

Draw an arc from P (again the same radius) and complete the angle

**b)** Use a ruler and a pair of compasses only to construct an angle of 90°.

**Solution**

Draw a line and mark a point A on the line. Draw two equal arcs from A to cross the line at P and Q

Draw an arc from P of a longer radius than the two arcs already drawn

Draw an arc from Q (same radius as that drawn from P) and complete the angle

---

## Example 3

**a)** Draw a line *AB*. Construct the **perpendicular bisector** of the line *AB*.

**Solution**

Draw a line *AB*. Draw long arcs of equal radius from points *A* and *B* to intersect at points *C* and *D*

Join *CD* to form the perpendicular bisector

**b)** Draw a line *AB*. Construct a perpendicular from a point *O* above the line.

**Solution**

Draw a line *AB*. Draw two arcs from *O* to cross *AB* at *P* and *Q*, then draw an arc from *P*

Draw an arc from *Q* using the same radius as that used for the arc from *P* and complete the perpendicular

**c)** Draw an angle. Construct the angle bisector.

**Solution**

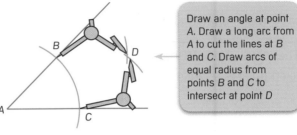

Draw an angle at point *A*. Draw a long arc from *A* to cut the lines at *B* and *C*. Draw arcs of equal radius from points *B* and *C* to intersect at point *D*

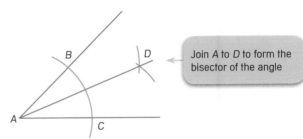

Join *A* to *D* to form the bisector of the angle

**d)** Construct an angle of 30°.

**Solution**

| Problem Solving |
| --- |
| Think about how you can combine basic constructions. In this case, construct an angle of 60° and then bisect it to create an angle half the size. |

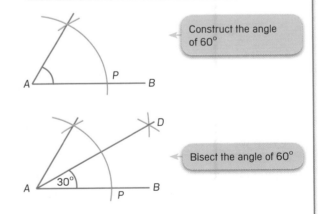

Construct the angle of 60°

Bisect the angle of 60°

## Quick Test

1. Construct a triangle *ABC* with *AB* = 8 cm, *BC* = 6.5 cm and *AC* = 5.7 cm

2. Construct an angle of 45°.

# Loci and 3-D Coordinates

## Loci

A **locus** (plural: **loci**) is a path made by a set of points that follow a rule.

Here are some facts about loci:

| | |
|---|---|
| The locus of points that are a fixed distance from a fixed point is a circle. 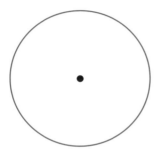 | The locus of points that are a fixed distance from a fixed line is a pair of parallel lines with a semicircle at either end. 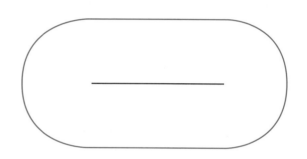 |
| The locus of points that are a fixed distance from two fixed points is the perpendicular bisector of the line joining the points. 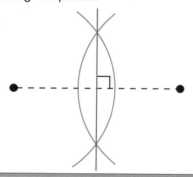 | The locus of points that are a fixed distance from two fixed lines is the angle bisector of the two lines. 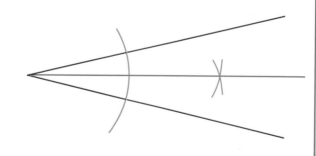 |

### Example

A goat is tied to the corner of a building by a rope 5 metres long. Show the area that the goat can reach on the diagram.

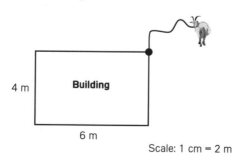

4 m    **Building**

6 m

Scale: 1 cm = 2 m

**Solution**

4 m    **Building**

6 m

This arc is of radius 5 metres

This arc is of radius 1 metre as 4 metres of the rope are along the side of the building

## 3-D Coordinates

You need to know that:

- **2-D coordinates** are used to identify points in a plane, using $x$ and $y$-axes
- **3-D coordinates** are used to identify points in space, using $x$, $y$ and $z$-axes.

The axes are drawn at right angles to each other as shown.

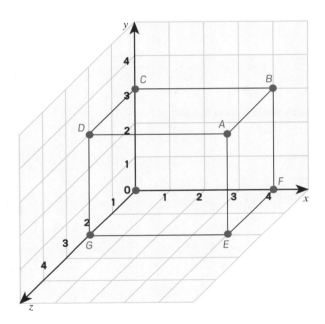

A has coordinates (4, 3, 2) because it's 4 units on the $x$-axis, 3 units on the $y$-axis and 2 units on the $z$-axis.

C has coordinates (0, 3, 0) because it's 0 units on the $x$-axis, 3 units on the $y$-axis and 0 units on the $z$-axis.

E has coordinates (4, 0, 2) because it's 4 units on the $x$-axis, 0 units on the $y$-axis and 2 units on the $z$-axis.

### Quick Test

1. A goat is tied to a post in each field by a rope 5 metres long. In each case describe or draw the locus of the shape the goat can reach. On the diagrams, 1 cm = 2 m

   a)

   b)

   c)

2. Look again at the diagram for 3-D coordinates on the left of this page and write down the coordinates of:

   a) F

   b) B

   c) G

   d) D

# Exam Practice Questions

You may wish to answer these questions on a separate piece of paper so that you can show full working out, which you will be expected to do in the exam.

Questions labelled with an asterisk (*) are ones where the quality of your written communication (QWC) will be assessed.

**1.** Work out the area of the trapezium. **(2)**

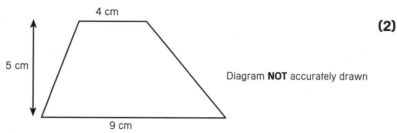

Diagram **NOT** accurately drawn

**2.**

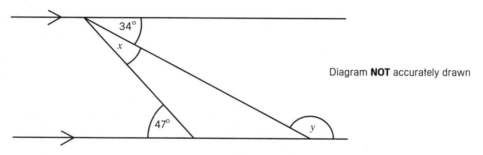

Diagram **NOT** accurately drawn

**a)** Work out the value of $x$. **(2)**

**b)** Work out the value of $y$. **(2)**

**3.** Work out the area of a circle of radius 4 cm. Give your answer in $cm^2$ to 1 decimal place. **(3)**

**4.** A ship sails 20 miles north from a port ($P$) to a lighthouse ($L$).

It then turns and sails 25 miles east to an oil rig ($R$). It then returns directly to the port.

**a)** Make a sketch of the route sailed by the ship. **(2)**

**b)** Work out the distance from the oil rig back to the port. Give your answer to a suitable degree of accuracy. **(3)**

**5.**

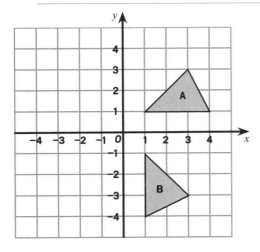

Describe fully the single transformation that maps triangle A to triangle B. **(3)**

**6.** Construct a triangle ABC with AB = 3 cm, angle BAC = 50° and angle ABC = 30° **(3)**

**7.** The diagram shows a solid metal cylinder and an open cuboid.

The cylinder is melted down and the metal is poured into the cuboid.

Work out the height of the metal in the cuboid. **(5)**

Diagram **NOT** accurately drawn

**\*8.** *A*, *B* and *D* are points on the circumference of the circle.

Triangle *BCD* is isosceles.

Diagram **NOT** accurately drawn

Work out the value of *x*. Give reasons for your answer. **(5)**

**\*9.** Work out the size of the smallest angle in this triangle. **(4)**

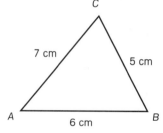

Diagram **NOT** accurately drawn

**10.** Work out the length of *BC*. **(4)**

Diagram **NOT** accurately drawn

**11.** The diagram shows a rectangle. The area is 27 cm².

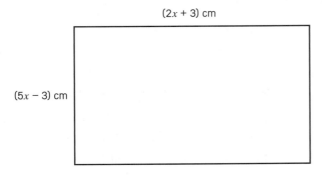

(2x + 3) cm

(5x − 3) cm

Diagram **NOT** accurately drawn

**a)** Show that $10x^2 + 9x - 36 = 0$ **(3)**

**b)** Solve the quadratic equation $10x^2 + 9x - 36 = 0$ **(3)**

**c)** Work out the length of the longest side of the rectangle. **(1)**

**12.** Give a reason why this pair of triangles is congruent. **(1)**

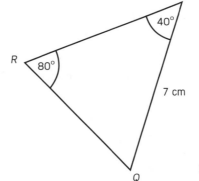

Diagram **NOT** accurately drawn

# Handling Data Cycle and Questionnaires

## The Handling Data Cycle

**Statistics** is about the collection, organisation and interpretation of data.

A **hypothesis** is an idea or assumption which is then tested to decide whether it's true or false. To test a hypothesis the **handling data cycle** is used.

Specify the problem. Plan the collection of the data.

Collect the data.

Process and represent the data.

Interpret and discuss the results.

To use the handling data cycle:
- state a hypothesis, outlining the problem and planning the task
- plan the data collection and collect the data
- process the data using statistical calculations, e.g. mean and range (see page 92)
- interpret the data and make conclusions.

The final step includes reviewing the task, refining it and continuing the cycle if necessary.

## Data Collection

You need to know these terms:
- **Primary data** is data that you collect.
- **Secondary data** is data that has already been collected by someone else.
- **Discrete data** can only have certain values in a given range, e.g. number of goals scored: 0, 1, 2, 3, and so on. It's not possible to have half a goal!
- **Continuous data** can have any value within a given range, e.g. height of a person: 1.83… metres.
- A **survey** is an organised way of collecting data.
- A **questionnaire** is one way of carrying out a survey.

- **Observations** in an **experiment** are another way of carrying out a survey.
- A **population** is all the group you're investigating.
- A **sample** is a part of the population you're investigating.

To collect the data:
1. decide whether to use the population or a sample
2. carry out a survey or an experiment
3. record the results in a suitable way, e.g. use a tally chart or a frequency table.

## Processing and Representing the Data

To process and represent the data:
- a suitable average could be calculated (mode, median or mean)
- a suitable measure of spread could be calculated (range or interquartile range)
- suitable statistical charts, diagrams or graphs could be drawn.

**Key Words**    Hypothesis • Primary data • Secondary data • Discrete data • Continuous data

# Handling Data Cycle and Questionnaires

## Interpreting and Discussing Results

Results are interpreted and discussed in order to:
- make comparisons
- draw conclusions

- decide whether the hypothesis is true, not true or inconclusive
- decide whether to refine the hypothesis or continue with the cycle.

### Example

A farmer wants to compare two types of lettuce, A and B, to decide which is better. Describe the handling data cycle that he could use.

#### Solution

**Problem Solving**

Think about what he would want to know and how he would collect the data. Then set out the information in a logical way.

**State a hypothesis:**

Lettuce A grows faster than lettuce B.

**Plan the data collection and collect the data:**

Plant a tray of each seed and store in the same conditions to avoid **bias**.

After two weeks measure the plants and record the results.

**Process and represent the data:**
- Work out the mean height of lettuces in each tray.
- Work out the interquartile range of the heights of lettuces in each tray.

**Interpret and discuss the results:**
- Look at the results and compare the means and the interquartile ranges.
- Decide whether there are any significant differences by referring to the context of the hypothesis.
- State how to improve the cycle, e.g. use a larger sample of seeds or measure after a different period of time.

## Questionnaires

Any question written as part of a questionnaire for a survey should:
- be as simple as possible
- allow anyone asked to give an answer
- have responses that don't overlap and have no gaps
- not be a leading, personal or irrelevant question.

### Example

Here is a question from a questionnaire about eating out. Give two criticisms of the response section.

**How many times do you eat out each week?**
❏ 1–3      ❏ 3–6      ❏ More than 7

#### Solution

3 could be in the first or second box.  ← Response options overlap

It's not possible to answer 0 or 7 times.  ← Gaps in the response options

### Quick Test

1. Ali thinks that boys are better than girls at spelling in his class. How could he use the handling data cycle to test his hypothesis?
2. Criticise this question:
   *Do you agree that fast food is bad for you?*
   ❏ Yes  ❏ No

# Averages and Range

## Mode, Median, Mean and Range

An **average** is a measure used to represent a set of data. The most commonly used averages are:

- the **mode** – the most common value (**MO**de is **MO**st)
- the **median** – the middle value of the ordered data or halfway between the middle two values for an even number of values (**MeD**ian is **MiD**dle)
- **mean** – given by the formula:

$$\text{Mean} = \frac{\textbf{sum of the values}}{\textbf{number of values}}$$

(Me**AN** is add up **AN**d divide.)

The **range** measures the spread of the data.

$$\text{Range} = \textbf{biggest value} - \textbf{smallest value}$$

### Example

Find five numbers that have a range of 6 and a mean of 4.

**Solution**

| Problem Solving |
|---|
| Work out the sum of the numbers using the mean. Here the sum of the numbers is five times the mean as there are five numbers. |

Sum of the numbers is $4 \times 5 = 20$

Written in order the first and last numbers have a difference of 6.

2 ... ... ... 8 ← Trying 2 and 8 means the other three numbers add up to 10

So 2  3  3  4  8 works. ← There are lots of other answers. Can you find a different answer?

## Mode, Median, Mean and Range from a Frequency Table

The mode, median, mean and range can be worked out from a frequency table.

### Example

Work out the mode, median, mean and range of the number of children per family.

| Number of Children ($x$) | Frequency ($f$) | Frequency × Number of Children ($fx$) |
|---|---|---|
| 0 | 4 | 0 |
| 1 | 6 | 6 |
| 2 | 9 | 18 |
| 3 | 1 | 3 |
| | Total = 20 | Total = 27 |

**Solution**

The mode is the most common, which is 2 children per family.

The median is the middle of the 20 values, which is halfway between the 10th and 11th values.

Listing in order: 0, 0, 0, 0, 1, 1, 1, 1, 1, 1, 2, 2, 2, 2, 2, 2, 2, 2, 2, 3

10th value = 1, 11th value = 2, so median = 1.5 children per family

$$\text{Mean} = \frac{\text{sum of the values}}{\text{number of values}}$$

$$\text{Mean} = \frac{27}{20} = 1.35 \text{ children per family}$$

Range is $3 - 0 = 3$ children per family

# Averages and Range

## Grouped Data

The **modal class** is the class with the biggest frequency. The class containing the median is the class that contains the middle value. To estimate the mean, mid-values are used to represent each class.

### Example

| Recorded Temp., $T$ ($^\circ$C) | Frequency ($f$) | Mid-Temp. Values ($x$) | Frequency × Mid-Temp. Values ($fx$) |
|---|---|---|---|
| $10 \leqslant T < 15$ | 2 | 12.5 | 2 × 12.5 = 25 |
| $15 \leqslant T < 20$ | 4 | 17.5 | 4 × 17.5 = 70 |
| $20 \leqslant T < 25$ | 5 | 22.5 | 5 × 22.5 = 112.5 |
| $25 \leqslant T < 30$ | 8 | 27.5 | 8 × 27.5 = 220 |
| $30 \leqslant T < 35$ | 5 | 32.5 | 5 × 32.5 = 162.5 |
| | **Total = 24** | | **Total = 590** |

These are class intervals

These are halfway values for the class intervals

**a)** Work out the modal class, the class that contains the median and an estimate of the mean for the recorded temperatures.

### Solution

The modal class is $25^\circ$C $\leqslant T < 30^\circ$C

There are 24 temperatures altogether so the middle is halfway between the 12th and 13th temperatures.

The class containing these is $25^\circ$C $\leqslant T < 30^\circ$C

The individual temperatures aren't known so the mid-value of each group is used as an estimate.

Estimate of mean = $\dfrac{\text{total of recorded temperatures}}{\text{total frequency}}$

Estimate of mean is $\dfrac{590}{24}$ = 24.58$^\circ$C

**b)** Explain why it's not possible to work out the range.

### Solution

> **Problem Solving**
> Think about what you need to know to work out the range and what information is missing. Write your explanation clearly.

The lowest and highest temperatures aren't known, only that the lowest temperature is in the class $10^\circ$C $\leqslant T < 15^\circ$C and the highest temperature is in the class $30^\circ$C $\leqslant T < 35^\circ$C.

## Quick Test

1. Work out the mode, median, mean and range for this data.

| $x$ | $f$ |
|---|---|
| 3 | 1 |
| 4 | 9 |
| 5 | 6 |
| 6 | 4 |

2. Work out the modal class, the class that contains the median and an estimate of the mean for this data.

| $x$ | $f$ |
|---|---|
| $0 < x \leqslant 2$ | 10 |
| $2 < x \leqslant 4$ | 21 |
| $4 < x \leqslant 6$ | 13 |
| $6 < x \leqslant 8$ | 7 |

# Sorting Data and Sampling Methods

## Stem and Leaf Diagrams

A **stem and leaf diagram** is used to sort discrete data into **ordered** groups. Numbers in the **stem** (often the 'tens' digits) and numbers in the **leaves** (often the 'units' digits) are aligned to show the shape of the distribution.

> ### Example
>
> A student records the number of text messages she sends each day for 15 days.
>
> | 21 | 32 | 31 | 10 | 18 | 19 | 25 | 37 |
> |----|----|----|----|----|----|----|----|
> | 30 | 34 | 22 | 25 | 34 | 32 | 25 |    |
>
> **a)** Show the results in a stem and leaf diagram.
>
> **Solution A**
>
> 10, 18, 19, 21, 22, 25, 25,  ← Sort the numbers into order
> 25, 30, 31, 32, 32, 34, 34, 37
>
> Stem    Leaves
>
> ```
> 1 | 0  8  9
> 2 | 1  2  5  5 (5)     ← Put the data into a stem and leaf diagram
> 3 | 0  1  2  2  4  4  7
> ```
>
> 1 | 0  represents 10 text messages  ← Add a key
>
> **Solution B**
>
> ```
> 1 | 0  8  9
> 2 | 1  5  2  5  5       ← Put the data into an unordered stem and leaf diagram
> 3 | 2  1  7  0  4  4  2
> ```
>
> ```
> 1 | 0  8  9
> 2 | 1  2  5  5 (5)      ← Reorder the values
> 3 | 0  1  2  2  4  4  7
> ```
>
> 1 | 0  represents 10 text messages  ← Add a key
>
>
>
> **b)** Work out the median.
>
> **Solution**
>
> The median of the 15 values is the 8th number (circled) when the numbers are ordered, so median = 25

## Two-way Tables

A **two-way table** is a table that links two sets of information.

The table shows there are 83 boys and 62 girls in year 10 and 75 boys and 94 girls in year 11.

|       | Year 10 | Year 11 |
|-------|---------|---------|
| Boys  | 83      | 75      |
| Girls | 62      | 94      |

**Key Words**        Stem and leaf diagram • Two-way table

## Example

Complete the two-way table using this information about people visiting a theatre:

- Altogether there are 120 adults.
- There are twice as many male adults as female adults.
- Altogether there are 75 females.
- There are 65 male children.

|  | Male | Female | Total |
|---|---|---|---|
| **Adults** |  |  |  |
| **Children** |  |  |  |
| **Total** |  |  |  |

### Solution

| Problem Solving |
|---|
| First fill in the numbers you're given (in this case 120, 65 and 75). Now calculate the missing ones. You're given the total number of adults and the proportion of male adults to female adults, so you can use ratio to find these. |

|  | Male | Female | Total |
|---|---|---|---|
| **Adults** | 80 | 40 | 120 |
| **Children** | 65 | 35 | 100 |
| **Total** | 145 | 75 | 220 |

120 divided in the ratio 2 : 1 = 80 : 40

## Sampling Methods

There are two main ways of sampling a population:

- **Random sampling** – every member of the population has an equal chance of being chosen.
- **Stratified sampling** – the population is divided into categories and the sample is taken using the same proportion in each category as in the population.

To obtain a random sample:

1 give every member of the population a number
2 choose numbers at random, e.g. by picking from a hat.

To obtain a stratified sample:

1 decide the categories to stratify
2 work out the same proportion of each category that gives the correct sample size overall.

## Example

There are 43 boys and 57 girls in a year group. A 10% sample stratified by gender is to be chosen for a committee. How many boys and how many girls are on the committee?

### Solution

10% of 43 is 4.3; 10% of 57 is 5.7

So 4 boys and 6 girls are chosen.

*Use whole numbers to obtain 10% of the total population*

## Quick Test

1 a) Show these lengths in an ordered stem and leaf diagram. Remember to complete a key.

   12 cm    14 cm    28 cm    25 cm
   22 cm    11 cm    12 cm    15 cm
   18 cm    25 cm    12 cm

   b) Work out the mode, median and range.

2 The two-way table shows the number of left-handed and right-handed boys and girls in a class.

|  | Left-handed | Right-handed |
|---|---|---|
| **Boys** | 5 | 8 |
| **Girls** | 6 | 10 |

   a) How many boys are in the class?
   b) A child is chosen at random. What is the probability it's a left-handed girl?

3 There are 36 managers, 23 secretaries and 81 manual workers in a factory. A 5% stratified sample is to be chosen by job type for a pay rise. How many of each type will be chosen?

# Representing Data

## Graphs and Charts

### Vertical Line Graphs and Bar Charts

A **vertical line graph** or a **bar chart** can be used to represent discrete data. The height of each line shows the frequency.

### Line Graphs

A **line graph** can be used for discrete or continuous data. If the values between the plots have no meaning, the points should be joined with a dashed line as shown.

### Multiple and Composite Bar Charts

A **multiple bar chart** and a **composite bar chart** show two or more groups of data:

- A multiple bar chart shows two or more groups of data side by side.
- A composite bar chart combines two or more groups of data into a single bar.

A **key** is needed for each group of data.

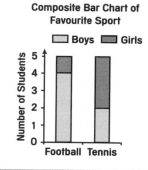

### Histograms and Frequency Polygons

A **histogram** or a **frequency polygon** can be used to show continuous data.

### Pie Charts

A **pie chart** can be used to show how parts of a whole are made up. Each part is represented by a sector of a circle. The angle of each sector is proportional to the frequency it represents.

This table of data has been used to create a pie chart.

| Favourite Sport | Number of Students | Calculation | Angle |
|---|---|---|---|
| Football | 7 | $\frac{7}{18} \times 360°$ | 140° |
| Tennis | 3 | $\frac{3}{18} \times 360°$ | 60° |
| Hockey | 8 | $\frac{8}{18} \times 360°$ | 160° |
| Total = 18 | | Total = 360° | |

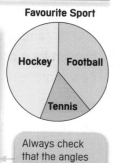

Always check that the angles add up to 360°

## Example

The frequency polygons show the lengths of time some students spend on a piece of work. Compare the times for boys and girls.

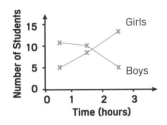

**Solution**

More girls spent longer on the task.

The total time for girls was approximately
(5 × 0.5 + 8 × 1.5 + 13 × 2.5) hours = 47 hours

The total time for boys was approximately
(11 × 0.5 + 10 × 1.5 + 5 × 2.5) hours = 33 hours

> **Problem Solving**
>
> Write down any true facts but ensure you compare the same facts for boys and girls.

## Scatter Diagrams

A **scatter diagram** (**scatter graph**) helps to compare two sets of data by plotting points to represent each pair of variables. **Correlation** describes any trend shown.

As temperature increases, ice-cream sales increase

As distance travelled increases, petrol remaining decreases

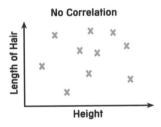

As height increases, there is no trend for length of hair

## Line of Best Fit

A **line of best fit**:

- is a straight line through the points
- can be used to estimate unknown values within the range of the points plotted
- is to show the trend – it doesn't have to pass exactly through any of the points.

The correlation is:

- **strong** if the points are very **close** to a line of best fit
- **weak** if the points are more widely **spread**.

## Quick Test

1. Draw a pie chart to show the number of people using a shop one day.

| Men | Women | Children |
|-----|-------|----------|
| 36 | 45 | 9 |

2. The table shows the time taken and the distance travelled on eight journeys.

| Distance (miles) | Time (minutes) |
|------------------|----------------|
| 1.4 | 3 |
| 7.2 | 15 |
| 5.0 | 8 |
| 3.6 | 6 |
| 8.4 | 13 |
| 9.3 | 12 |
| 2.4 | 5 |
| 6.4 | 11 |

   a) Plot the data on a scatter graph.
   b) Draw a line of best fit.
   c) Estimate the time taken for a journey of 4 miles.

3. Draw a frequency polygon for this data of the time taken to complete a task.

| Time, $t$ (minutes) | Frequency |
|---------------------|-----------|
| $0 < t \leqslant 20$ | 3 |
| $20 < t \leqslant 40$ | 5 |
| $40 < t \leqslant 60$ | 2 |

# Further Ways of Representing Data

## Cumulative Frequency Diagrams and Box Plots

### Cumulative Frequency Diagrams

To draw a **cumulative frequency** graph:

1. work out the running totals of the frequencies
2. plot these totals against the upper class boundaries
3. join the points with either straight lines (cumulative frequency polygon) or a curve (cumulative frequency curve).

Always check that the last running total is the same as the total frequency for the question.

A cumulative frequency graph can be used to work out:

- the median of the data — read off from halfway up the total frequency
- the **lower quartile** — read off from a quarter of the way up the total frequency
- the **upper quartile** — read off from three-quarters of the way up the total frequency
- the **interquartile range**, i.e.
  upper quartile value — lower quartile value
- the proportion or amount of the data that is above or below a particular value.

### Box Plots

**Box plots** use five key values of the data, namely the minimum value, lower quartile, median, upper quartile and the maximum value.

#### Example 1

The table shows the time taken for 80 students to travel to school. The shortest time taken is 2 minutes and the longest time taken is 60 minutes.

Draw a cumulative frequency graph and use this to draw a box plot.

| Time Taken, $T$ (minutes) | Frequency (i.e. no. of students) | Cumulative Frequency |
|---|---|---|
| $0 < T \leqslant 10$ | 5 | 5 |
| $10 < T \leqslant 20$ | 9 | (9 + 5 = ) 14 |
| $20 < T \leqslant 30$ | 16 | (16 + 14 = ) 30 |
| $30 < T \leqslant 40$ | 29 | (29 + 30 = ) 59 |
| $40 < T \leqslant 50$ | 15 | (15 + 59 = ) 74 |
| $50 < T \leqslant 60$ | 6 | (6 + 74 = ) 80 |

This matches the total given in the question

**Solution**

Using the upper class boundaries, plot the points (2, 0), (10, 5), (20, 14), (30, 30), (40, 59), (50, 74) and (60, 80)

The median is 34 minutes. The lower quartile is 24 minutes and the upper quartile is 41 minutes

**Key Words** Cumulative frequency • Lower quartile • Upper quartile • Interquartile range • Box plot

# Further Ways of Representing Data

**Example 2**

Use the cumulative frequency graph in Example 1 to work out the percentage of students who take longer than 25 minutes to get to school.

**Solution**

| Problem Solving |
| --- |
| You can read off at 25 minutes to see how many students took 25 minutes or less. You can then work out how many took more than 25 minutes and then change this to a percentage. |

Reading off at 25 minutes gives 21 students, so $80 - 21 = 59$ students took longer than 25 minutes.

59 as a percentage of 80 is $\frac{59}{80} \times 100 = 74\%$

## Histograms

A **histogram** is used to show continuous data.

The **area** of each bar represents the **frequency** for that bar. When the class widths aren't the same the vertical axis is the **frequency density**. So:

| Area of bar (frequency of class interval) | = | frequency density | × | width of class interval |
| --- | --- | --- | --- | --- |

| Frequency density | = | frequency of class interval / width of class interval |
| --- | --- | --- |

*Frequency **D**ensity = **F**requency **D**ivided by class width*

| Age, $A$ (years) | Frequency | Frequency Density |
| --- | --- | --- |
| $0 < A \leqslant 10$ | 10 | 1 |
| $10 < A \leqslant 20$ | 20 | 2 |
| $20 < A \leqslant 30$ | 60 | 6 |
| $30 < A \leqslant 40$ | 50 | 5 |
| $40 < A \leqslant 60$ | 60 | 3 |
| $60 < A \leqslant 100$ | 20 | 0.5 |

## Quick Test

1. The test marks of 80 students are shown.

| Mark, $x$ | Number of Students | Cumulative Frequency |
| --- | --- | --- |
| $0 < x \leqslant 10$ | 6 | 6 |
| $10 < x \leqslant 20$ | 12 | 18 |
| $20 < x \leqslant 30$ | 19 | |
| $30 < x \leqslant 40$ | 26 | |
| $40 < x \leqslant 50$ | 13 | |
| $50 < x \leqslant 60$ | 4 | |

a) Complete the table.
b) Draw a cumulative frequency graph.
c) Work out the median and the interquartile range.
d) The lowest mark was 4 and the highest mark was 55. Draw a box plot to show the data.

2. Draw a histogram for this grouped frequency distribution:

| Height, $h$ (cm) | Frequency |
| --- | --- |
| $100 < h \leqslant 102$ | 8 |
| $102 < h \leqslant 103$ | 6 |
| $103 < h \leqslant 107$ | 20 |
| $107 < h \leqslant 110$ | 9 |

**Represents 10 people**

The key is useful but not expected or asked for in the exam

**Key Words**          Histogram • Frequency density          99

# Probability

## Probability Facts

You need to know the following:

- An **event** is anything that you want to use to measure the probability of something happening, e.g. tossing a coin.
- An **outcome** is the result of an event, e.g. getting a head.

- P(A) means the probability of outcome A happening.
- **Equally likely outcomes** each have the same probability of happening, e.g. getting a head or a tail on a fair coin.

## Probability of an Outcome

$$P(\text{outcome}) = \frac{\text{number of ways the outcome can happen}}{\text{total number of possible outcomes}}$$

### Example

There are 8 boys and 7 girls in a team. The captain is chosen at random.

Write down the probability the captain is a girl.

**Solution**

There are 7 girls out of 15 in the team, so $P(\text{girl}) = \frac{7}{15}$

## Mutually Exclusive Events

**Mutually exclusive events** are events that have no outcomes in common, e.g. choosing an odd or an even number from a list.

If two events A and B are mutually exclusive:

$$P(A \text{ or } B) = P(A) + P(B)$$

If the probability of an outcome is $p$, the probability of the outcome not happening is $1 - p$.

### Example

In a drawer there are only blue and black socks. The probability of picking a black sock at random is $\frac{3}{5}$.

**a)** What is the probability of picking a blue sock?

**Solution**

$P(\text{blue})$ is $1 - P(\text{black}) = 1 - \frac{3}{5} = \frac{2}{5}$

**b)** There are 4 more black socks than blue socks. How many socks are in the drawer altogether?

**Solution**

> **Problem Solving**
>
> Start by working out what fraction 4 socks is of all the socks in the drawer. You can then use this fraction to work out the total number of socks.

The probability of picking a black sock is $\frac{1}{5}$ greater than picking a blue sock. So the extra 4 socks must represent $\frac{3}{5} - \frac{2}{5} = \frac{1}{5}$ of the total socks in the drawer.

So there are $4 \times 5$

= 20 socks in the drawer  ←  12 black and 8 blue

## Combined Events

A **sample space diagram** can be used to show the possible outcomes from two events, e.g. tossing a coin and throwing a dice.

| | | Dice | | | | | |
|---|---|---|---|---|---|---|---|
| | | 1 | 2 | 3 | 4 | 5 | 6 |
| Coin | Head | Head, 1 | Head, 2 | Head, 3 | Head, 4 | Head, 5 | Head, 6 |
| | Tail | Tail, 1 | Tail, 2 | Tail, 3 | Tail, 4 | Tail, 5 | Tail, 6 |

$P(\text{Head and } 3) = \frac{1}{12}$

$P(\text{Tail and odd}) \text{ is } \frac{3}{12} = \frac{1}{4}$

## Independent Events

Two events are **independent** if the outcome of one event isn't affected by the outcome of the other event.

If two events A and B are independent:

$$P(A \text{ and } B) = P(A) \times P(B)$$

### Example 1

A coin is tossed twice. Work out the probability of getting two heads.

**Solution**

**Problem Solving**

Tossing a coin twice represents two independent events, so $P(A \text{ and } B) = P(A) \times P(B)$ is the formula to use here. Alternatively you could use a sample space diagram.

$P(HH) = P(H) \times P(H)$

$= \frac{1}{2} \times \frac{1}{2}$

$= \frac{1}{4}$

### Example 2

A fair coin is tossed and a fair dice is thrown. Work out the probability of getting a tail and a 3.

**Solution**

$P(\text{Tail and } 3) = P(\text{Tail}) \times P(3)$

$= \frac{1}{2} \times \frac{1}{6}$

$= \frac{1}{12}$

Same answer as using a sample space diagram

## Quick Test

1. Write down the probabilities of the following:
   a) A fair coin landing on heads.  b) Rolling a 1 or a 2 on a fair dice.  c) Rolling a 7 on a fair dice.
2. Two fair dice are rolled. Work out the probability of a total score of 7.

# Further Probability

## Conditional Probability

**Conditional probability** describes the probability of events whose outcomes aren't independent. This is sometimes known as **probability without replacement**.

### Example

A bag contains six coloured counters. Two are yellow and four are blue.

A counter is taken out and not replaced.

Another is then taken out. ← *This is the same as taking two out together*

Work out the probability that:

**a)** the first counter is blue

**Solution**

Four of the six counters are blue

So P(First counter blue) is $\frac{4}{6} = \frac{2}{3}$

**b)** both counters are blue.

**Solution**

If the first counter was blue, there are now two yellow and three blue counters left.

So P(Second counter blue) is $\frac{3}{5}$

So P(Both counters blue) is $\frac{2}{3} \times \frac{3}{5} = \frac{6}{15} = \frac{2}{5}$

## Tree Diagrams

A **tree diagram** can be used as an alternative method for dealing with problems involving two or more events. The tree diagram has **branches** to show each event.

### Example 1

A coin is tossed twice. Use a tree diagram to work out the probability of getting:

**a)** two heads

**Solution**

P(HH) = P(H) × P(H) = $\frac{1}{4}$

**b)** at least one tail.

**Solution**

P(At least one tail) = 1 − P(HH) = $\frac{3}{4}$

*Or P(At least one tail) = P(HT) + P(TH) + P(TT) = $\frac{3}{4}$*

| | Outcome | Probability |
|---|---|---|
| $\frac{1}{2}$ H | (H, H) | $\frac{1}{2} \times \frac{1}{2} = \frac{1}{4}$ |
| $\frac{1}{2}$ T | (H, T) | $\frac{1}{2} \times \frac{1}{2} = \frac{1}{4}$ |
| $\frac{1}{2}$ H | (T, H) | $\frac{1}{2} \times \frac{1}{2} = \frac{1}{4}$ |
| $\frac{1}{2}$ T | (T, T) | $\frac{1}{2} \times \frac{1}{2} = \frac{1}{4}$ |

**Example 2**

A fruit bowl has three red and four green apples. Two apples are chosen at random.

Use a tree diagram to work out the probability of two red apples being chosen.

**Solution**

Looking at the tree diagram:

$P(RR) = P(R) \times P(R)$

$= \frac{3}{7} \times \frac{2}{6}$

$= \frac{1}{7}$

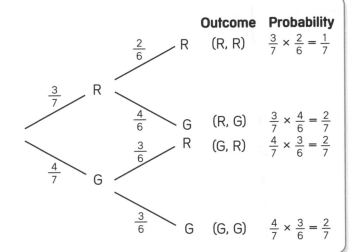

| | Outcome | Probability |
|---|---|---|
| R | (R, R) | $\frac{3}{7} \times \frac{2}{6} = \frac{1}{7}$ |
| G | (R, G) | $\frac{3}{7} \times \frac{4}{6} = \frac{2}{7}$ |
| R | (G, R) | $\frac{4}{7} \times \frac{3}{6} = \frac{2}{7}$ |
| G | (G, G) | $\frac{4}{7} \times \frac{3}{6} = \frac{2}{7}$ |

## Theoretical Probability, Relative Frequency and Expectation

Probability based on:

- equally likely outcomes is called **theoretical probability**, e.g. P(Head on a fair coin) = $\frac{1}{2}$, as it's assumed that there are two equally likely outcomes (heads and tails)
- the results of an experiment is called **experimental probability** or **relative frequency**:

$$\text{Relative frequency} = \frac{\text{frequency of a particular outcome}}{\text{total number of trials}}$$

More trials should give a more reliable result.

**Expectation** is the number of times you would expect an event to happen based on the relative frequency or theoretical probability.

**Quick Test**

1. In a bag there are three red, four blue and three white counters. One counter is chosen at random. A second counter is then chosen at random. Work out the probability that both counters were red:
   a) if the first counter was replaced
   b) if the first counter wasn't replaced.

**Example**

A five-sided spinner is spun 100 times. Here are the results:

| 1 | 2 | 3 | 4 | 5 |
|---|---|---|---|---|
| 16 | 23 | 32 | 12 | 17 |

a) Write down the relative frequency of landing on the number 4.

**Solution**

The spinner lands on the number 4 twelve times out of 100, so the relative frequency is $\frac{12}{100}$

b) Do you think the spinner is biased? Give a reason for your answer.

**Problem Solving**

Compare the relative frequency with the theoretical probability or look at the expectation for the outcomes based on theoretical probability.

**Solution**

If the spinner is fair, you would expect it to land on each number 20 times (out of 100) but here it lands on 3 thirty-two times. So it appears the spinner is biased because it's more likely to land on 3 than on the other numbers.

# Exam Practice Questions

You may wish to answer these questions on a separate piece of paper so that you can show full working out, which you will be expected to do in the exam.

Questions labelled with an asterisk (*) are ones where the quality of your written communication (QWC) will be assessed.

1. A bag contains white, blue and red counters.

   A counter is chosen at random from the bag.

   The probability of choosing white is double the probability of choosing red.

   The probability of choosing blue is three times the probability of choosing red.

   a) Work out the probability that a red counter is chosen. **(3)**

   b) Jon says that there are exactly 10 counters in the bag. Explain why he must be wrong. **(1)**

2. The scatter graph shows the number of driving tests taken to pass and the number of hours of lessons for 13 students.

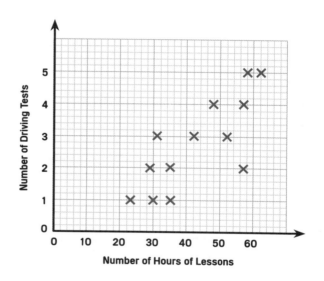

   Copy the graph.

   a) One of the students had more hours than normal for the number of tests taken. Circle this point on the graph and give a reason why it should be ignored. **(2)**

   b) Draw a line of best fit on your graph. **(1)**

   c) Describe the relationship between the number of tests taken to pass and the number of hours of lessons. **(1)**

**3.** When driving to the shops, I go through two sets of traffic lights.

The probability that I stop at the first set is $\frac{1}{4}$. The probability that I stop at the second set is $\frac{2}{3}$.

**a)** Copy and complete the tree diagram to show the possible outcomes when going through the two sets of lights. **(2)**

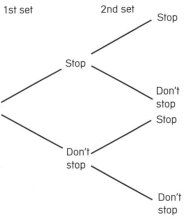

**b)** Work out the probability that I stop at both sets of lights. **(2)**

**4.** The box plots show information about the midday temperatures for two holiday towns in September.

Compare the temperatures in town A and town B. **(2)**

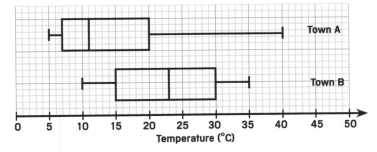

**5.** The table shows the weights of 240 parcels collected by a courier.

| Weight, $w$ (grams) | Frequency |
|---|---|
| $0 < w \leqslant 100$ | 40 |
| $100 < w \leqslant 300$ | 64 |
| $300 < w \leqslant 500$ | 86 |
| $500 < w \leqslant 1000$ | 50 |

**\*a)** Draw a fully labelled histogram on a piece of graph paper to show this information. **(3)**

**b)** On the following day, the courier collected 500 parcels. Use the data in the table to estimate the number of parcels that weighed 100 grams or less. **(3)**

# Answers

## Quick Tests

### Rounding (pages 4–5)

1. **a)** **i)** 18.7 **ii)** 18.73
   **iii)** 20 **iv)** 19
   **b)** **i)** 0.1 **ii)** 0.07
   **iii)** 0.07 **iv)** 0.073
   **c)** **i)** 2436.5 **ii)** 2436.52
   **iii)** 2000 **iv)** 2400
2. **a)** 10 **b)** 20 **c)** 2000

### Multiples and Factors (pages 6–7)

1. **a)** 14 **b)** 130 **c)** 75
2. $60 = 2 \times 2 \times 3 \times 5 = 2^2 \times 3 \times 5$
3. **a)** 40 **b)** 28 **c)** 18
4. **a)** 4 **b)** 5 **c)** 6

### Fractions (pages 8–9)

1. **a)** $4\frac{7}{12}$ **b)** $1\frac{7}{20}$
   **c)** 2 **d)** $1\frac{49}{65}$
2. £40
3. $\frac{1}{20}$

### Percentages (pages 10–11)

1. 180 grams
2. 8.33% or $8\frac{1}{3}$%
3. **a)** £16.80 **b)** 78 minutes
4. £1125 (to nearest pound)
5. 15

### Powers and Roots (pages 12–13)

1. **a)** 144 **b)** 27
   **c)** 13 **d)** 10
2. **a)** 6 **b)** 5
   **c)** $\frac{1}{2}$ **d)** $\frac{1}{9}$

### Standard Index Form (pages 14–15)

1. **a)** $3.72 \times 10^2$ **b)** $6 \times 10^3$
   **c)** $2.3 \times 10^{-2}$ **d)** $5.67 \times 10^0$
2. **a)** 314 **b)** 21 000
   **c)** 0.365 **d)** 0.058
3. **a)** 2060 or $2.06 \times 10^3$
   **b)** $-1590$ or $-1.59 \times 10^3$
   **c)** 2 418 000 or $2.418 \times 10^6$
   **d)** $5 \times 10^{-4}$

### Ratio (pages 16–17)

1. **a)** 1 : 7 **b)** 3 : 2
   **c)** 1 : 20 **d)** 5 : 1
2. **a)** 1 : 2 **b)** 9
3. £16 and £20
4. 90 kg

### Proportion (pages 18–19)

1. 12
2. $138.\dot{8}$

### Upper and Lower Bounds (pages 20–21)

1. **a)** Upper 54, lower 45
   **b)** Upper 50.5 mph, lower 49.5 mph
   **c)** Upper 52.5 cm, lower 47.5 cm
2. Slowest 7.61 m/s, fastest 7.78 m/s

### Recurring Decimals and Surds (pages 22–23)

1. **a)** 0.4 **b)** $0.\dot{4}$ **c)** $0.\dot{2}30769\dot{9}$
2. $\frac{7}{33}$
3. **a)** $3\sqrt{2}$ **b)** $14 + 6\sqrt{5}$
4. $4\sqrt{2}$

### Basic Algebra (pages 24–25)

1. **a)** $5x$ **b)** $-4x + 7y$
   **c)** $-2x^2 + 9xy$ **d)** $7x - z$
2. **a)** 5 **b)** $15\frac{1}{2}$ **c)** $-2\frac{1}{2}$
3. **a)** $x = \frac{5y}{2 - y}$ **b)** $x = \frac{3y + 2}{y - 1}$

### Expanding Brackets and Factorising (pages 26–27)

1. $10x + 15$
2. $x^2 - 2x - 15$
3. **a)** $4x(2x - 3)$ **b)** $(x - 1)(x - 2)$
   **c)** $(3x + 4)(x - 5)$ **d)** $(x - 4y)(x + 4y)$

### Linear Equations (pages 28–29)

1. **a)** $x = 3$ **b)** $x = 2$ **c)** $x = -1.25$
2. **a)** $x = -7$ **b)** $x = 2$ **c)** $x = 6$
3. **a)** $x = 3$ **b)** $x = 2.75$ **c)** $x = 4.33$

### Quadratic Equations (pages 30–31)

1. **a)** 2, 9 **b)** $-\frac{1}{3}$, 5
2. **a)** $3 \pm \sqrt{5}$ **b)** $\frac{-3 \pm \sqrt{53}}{2}$
3. **a)** 1.77, $-2.27$ **b)** 2.18, 0.15

### Trial and Improvement & Sequences (pages 32–33)

1. **a)** 2.7 **b)** 2.8 or 0.6 or $-3.4$
2. **a)** **i)** 20, 23 **ii)** $3n + 2$ **iii)** 62
   **b)** **i)** 30, 34 **ii)** $4n + 6$ **iii)** 86

### Straight Line Graphs (pages 34–35)

1. $\frac{3}{2}$, (0, 3)
2. $y = 3x + 1$ and $6x - 2y = 9$ both have gradient = 3, so are parallel.
   $x = 3y + 1$ has gradient = $\frac{1}{3}$, and $3x + y = 4$ has gradient = $-3$, so these are perpendicular.

### Linear Inequalities (pages 36–37)

1. **a)**
   **b)**
2. **a)** $x > 4$ **b)** $x \geqslant 1.5$
3.

## Simultaneous Equations (pages 38–39)

1. $x = 5, y = 1$
2. $x = 4, y = 1$ and $x = -1, y = -4$

## Harder Equations and Graphs (pages 40–41)

1.

2. a)  b)  c)

## Trigonometrical Graphs and Transformations (pages 42–43)

1.

2. Translation of $90°$ in the $x$-direction.

## Angles and Parallel Lines (pages 48–49)

1. a) $126°$; allied angles
   b) $47°$; angles on a straight line and alternate (or corresponding) angles
   c) $21°$; angles on a straight line and alternate (or corresponding) angles

## Angles of Polygons (pages 50–51)

1. a) Exterior $45°$, interior $135°$
   b) Exterior $36°$, interior $144°$

## Areas of Triangles and Quadrilaterals (pages 52–53)

1. a) $8.05 \text{ cm}^2$   b) $12.65 \text{ cm}^2$
   c) $10.08 \text{ cm}^2$   d) $8.94 \text{ cm}^2$

## Circumference and Area of Circles (pages 54–55)

1. a) i) $29.5$ cm   ii) $69.4 \text{ cm}^2$
   b) i) $19.2$ cm   ii) $29.2 \text{ cm}^2$
   c) i) $15.1$ cm   ii) $18.1 \text{ cm}^2$
2. a) i) $10\pi$ cm   ii) $25\pi \text{ cm}^2$
   b) i) $12\pi$ cm   ii) $36\pi \text{ cm}^2$

## Arc Length and Area of a Sector (pages 56–57)

1. a) i) $12.0$ cm   ii) $36.1 \text{ cm}^2$
   b) i) $6.6$ cm   ii) $29.7 \text{ cm}^2$
   c) i) $13.3$ cm   ii) $26.5 \text{ cm}^2$

## Plan and Elevation (pages 58–59)

1. a) i)  ii) iii)
   b) i)  ii) iii)
   c) i)  ii) iii)

(Accept elevations in either order)

## Volumes of Prisms (pages 60–61)

1. a) $60 \text{ cm}^3$   b) $491 \text{ cm}^3$   c) $42 \text{ cm}^3$

## Volumes of Pyramids, Cones and Spheres (pages 62–63)

1. a) $25.5 \text{ cm}^3$   b) $64.1 \text{ cm}^3$   c) $34.7 \text{ cm}^3$

## Pythagoras' Theorem (pages 64–65)

1. a) $17$ cm   b) $8.06$ cm   c) $6.24$ cm

## Surface Area (pages 66–67)

1. a) $54 \text{ cm}^2$   b) $62 \text{ cm}^2$   c) $132 \text{ cm}^2$
   d) $90\pi \text{ cm}^2$   e) $75.4 \text{ cm}^2$

## Trigonometry in Right-angled Triangles (pages 68–69)

1. a) $6.7$ cm   b) $11.4$ cm   c) $60°$

## Sine and Cosine Rules (pages 70–71)

1. a) $15.4$ cm   b) $38.7°$
   c) $6.58$ cm   d) $36.9°$

# Answers

## Circle Theorems (pages 72–73)

1. **a)** 32°     **b)** 56°
   **c)** 88°     **d)** 65°

## Transformations (pages 74–75)

1. **a)** A translation by the vector $\begin{pmatrix} 5 \\ -1 \end{pmatrix}$
   **b)** A reflection in the line $y = x$
   **c)** A rotation 90° anticlockwise about (0, 0)

## Congruency and Similarity (pages 76–77)

1. SAS
2. 4.8 cm
3. 8 : 27

## Vectors (pages 78–79)

1. **a)** $-\mathbf{b} + \mathbf{a}$     **b)** $\mathbf{a} - 3\mathbf{b}$     **c)** $-2\mathbf{a} + 4\mathbf{b}$
2. **a)** $\begin{pmatrix} 2 \\ 2 \end{pmatrix}$     **b)** $\begin{pmatrix} -1 \\ 4 \end{pmatrix}$

## Conversions, Bearings and Scale Drawings (pages 80–81)

1. **a)**      **b)**      **c)**

## Constructions (pages 82–83)

1. Triangle drawn to scale with lengths accurate to ±1 mm

2.

## Loci and 3-D Coordinates (pages 84–85)

1. **a)**

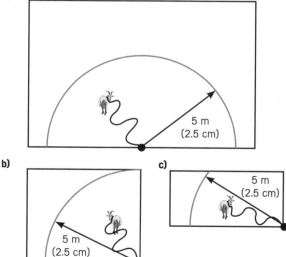

**b)**     **c)**

2. **a)** (4, 0, 0)     **b)** (4, 3, 0)
   **c)** (0, 0, 2)     **d)** (0, 3, 2)

## Handling Data Cycle and Questionnaires (pages 90–91)

1. **Any suitable answer, e.g.** Give each person 10 spellings; record the results; work out the mean number correct for boys and girls separately; compare the means and decide if there is any significant difference in the results.
2. It's a leading question as "Do you agree" is showing bias. It's not possible to say "Don't know".

## Averages and Range (pages 92–93)

1. Mode = 4; median = 4.5; mean = 4.65; range = 3
2. Modal class = $2 < x \le 4$; class containing median = $2 < x \le 4$; estimate of mean = 3.67

## Sorting Data and Sampling Methods (pages 94–95)

1. **a)**

   $\begin{array}{c|cccccc} 1 & 1 & 2 & 2 & 2 & 4 & 5 & 8 \\ 2 & 2 & 5 & 5 & 8 \end{array}$

   Key: 1 | 1 represents 11 cm

   **b)** Mode = 12 cm; median = 15 cm; range = 17 cm
2. **a)** 13     **b)** $\dfrac{6}{29}$
3. 2 managers, 1 secretary and 4 manual workers

## Representing Data (pages 96–97)

1. A pie chart should be drawn with angles of: Men 144°; Women 180°; Children 36°
2. **a) and b)**

   **c)** 7 minutes

3.

## Further Ways of Representing Data (pages 98–99)

1. **a)** 37, 63, 76, 80
   **b)**

   **c)** Median = 31, interquartile range = 16
   **d)**

2.

## Probability (pages 100–101)

1. **a)** $\frac{1}{2}$     **b)** $\frac{1}{3}$     **c)** 0
2. $\frac{1}{6}$

## Further Probability (pages 102–103)

1. **a)** $\frac{9}{100}$     **b)** $\frac{1}{15}$

## Exam Practice Questions

*Key: M are marks for method (e.g. **M1** means 1 mark for method); A are accuracy marks (e.g. **A1** means 1 mark for accuracy); B are independent marks that don't require method to be shown (e.g. **B2** means 2 independent marks); C are marks for quality of written communication (e.g. **C1** means 1 QWC mark).*

*You're encouraged to show your working out, as you may be awarded marks for method even if your final answer is wrong. Full marks can be awarded where a correct answer is given without working being shown but if a question asks for working out, you must show it to gain full marks. If you use a correct method that isn't shown in the mark scheme below, you would still gain full credit for it.*

## Number and Algebra (pages 44–47)

1. **M1 a)** $8 + 32x - 4x - 12 = 0$ **(One error allowed)**
   **M1**   $28x - 4 = 0$ or $28x = 4$
   **A1**   $x = \frac{1}{7}$
   **M1 b)** $\frac{y}{2} = 11 + 5$ or $\frac{y}{2} = 16$
   **A1**   $y = 32$

2. **M1** (Fridge World)
       $480 \div 3$ or £160
       or $480 - 160$
   **M1** (Fridge Bargains)
       $12 \times 25$ or £300
   **M1** (The Electric Store)
       $\frac{20}{100} \times 300$ or $0.2 \times 300$
       or £60
   **A2** £320, £340, £360 **(A1 for any two correct prices)**
   **C1** Fridge World (is the cheapest)

   *To score the quality of written communication mark you must have shown the method for each calculation.*

3. **M1 a)** $6^2 + 5$ or $36 + 5$
   **A1**   41
   **M1 b)** $7^2 + 5 = 54$ or $8^2 + 5 = 69$
       or $9^2 + 5 = 86$ or $10^2 + 5 = 105$
       or $11^2 + 5 = 126$
   **A1**   No, with working shown or reason given, e.g. $n^2 = 120$ doesn't give a whole number answer

   *There are lots of valid reasons for answering this part, e.g. 10th term = 105, 11th term = 126 or 125 isn't 5 more than a square number, it's 4 more than a square number.*

4. **M1** $7 + 5$ or 12 parts seen
   **M1** $84 \div 12$ or 1 part = £7
   **A1** 2 parts = £14
   **C1** She isn't correct

   *Must see working to award the quality of written communication mark.*

5. **M1 a)** $\frac{16\,500 - 6900}{3}$
   **A1** £3200
   **M1 b)** $6900 - 3200$
   **A1** £3700

6. **M1 a)** Lists multiples of 9 (9, 18, 27, 36, 45…) or writes $9 = 3 \times 3$
   **M1** Lists multiples of 15 (15, 30, 45…) or writes $15 = 3 \times 5$
   **A1** LCM = $3 \times 3 \times 5 = 45$
   **M1 b)** Factors of 36 = 1, 2, 3, 4, 6, 9, 12, 18, 36
   **M1** Factors of 60 = 1, 2, 3, 4, 5, 6, 10, 12, 15, 20, 30, 60
   **A1** HCF = 12

# Answers

**7.** **M1 a)** Factors of 42 shown, e.g. 42 = 6 × 7 or 42 = 3 × 14 or
42 = 2 × 21
May be on a factor tree:

 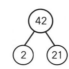

**A1** 2 × 3 × 7
**B1 b)** $2^2 × 3^2 × 7^2$

**8.** **M1 a)** Kylie has £$\frac{x}{2}$ or Jack has £($\frac{x}{2}$ + 5)

**A1** Kylie has £$\frac{x}{2}$ and Jack has £($\frac{x}{2}$ + 5)

So total 20 = $x + \frac{x}{2} + \frac{x}{2} + 5$

**M1 b)** 2x + 5 = 20
**M1** 2x = 20 − 5 or 2x = 15 or x = 7.5
**C1** £7.50 **(Money notation must be correct)**

**9.** **M1 a)** $3 + \frac{3}{12} + \frac{8}{12}$

**A1** $3\frac{11}{12}$

**M1 b)** $3\frac{1}{3} = \frac{10}{3}$ or $1\frac{1}{2} = \frac{3}{2}$

**M1** $\frac{10}{3} × \frac{3}{2}$

**A1** 5

**10.** **M1** 120% = £168
**M1** 168 ÷ 1.2 or 168 ÷ 120 × 100
**A1** £140

**11.** **B2 a)** $4y(2x − 3y)$ **(B1 for a partial factorisation $2y(4x − 6y)$
or $y(8x − 12y)$ or $4(2xy − 3y^2)$ or $2(4xy − 6y^2)$)**
**B2 b)** $(2x + 1)(x − 3)$ **(B1 for $(2x + a)(x + b)$ where $ab = ±3$)**

**12.** **M1 a)** 15 000 − 5040 or £9960
or 14 400 − 8100 or £6300

**M1** $\frac{20}{100}$ × 9960 or $\frac{20}{100}$ × 6300
**A1** £1992 and £1260
**C1** £1992 − £1260 = £732 and Harry

*Remember to answer the question by stating clearly who pays most tax.*

**M1 b)** 15 000 − 1992
or 14 400 − 1260
**C1** £13 008 and £13 140
Kim takes home £132 more.

*Remember to answer the question by stating clearly who takes home most pay.*

**13.** **B1 a)** 2
**M1 b)** $(\sqrt{9})^3$ or $3^3$
**A1** 27

**14.** **B1 a)** $1.4 × 10^6$
**B1 b)** 300 000 000

**15.** **M1** Gradient of y = 3x − 2 is 3

**M1** Gradient of perpendicular is $-\frac{1}{3}$

**A1** $y = -\frac{1}{3}x + 4$
or 3y = 4 − x or equivalent

**16.** **B1 a)**

**B1 b)** (−1, 0)

**17.** **M1** $I \propto \frac{1}{R}$ or $I = \frac{k}{R}$

**M1** $10 = \frac{k}{24}$ or k = 240

**A1** $I = \frac{240}{R}$

**C1** When R = 48, I = 5, so current halves

*Must state that I = 5 and current halves to award final mark.*

**18.** **M1 a)** $9 + 3\sqrt{5} + 3\sqrt{5} + 5$
**A1** $14 + 6\sqrt{5}$

**M1 b)** $\frac{10}{\sqrt{2}} × \frac{\sqrt{2}}{\sqrt{2}}$ or $\frac{10\sqrt{2}}{2}$

**A1** $5\sqrt{2}$

## Geometry and Measures (pages 86–89)

**1.** **M1** $\frac{1}{2}(9 + 4) × 5$
**A1** 32.5 cm²

**2.** **M1 a)** x + 34° = 47° or x = 47° − 34°
**A1** x = 13°
**M1 b)** y = 180° − 34° or y = 133° + 13°
**A1** y = 146°

**3.** **M1** π × 4 × 4 or π × 4²
**A1** 50.26…
**B1** 50.3 cm² **(Follow through any incorrect answer correctly
rounded to 1 d.p. Accept 50.2 cm² if π = 3.14 is used.)**

*It's important that you write down your answer to more than 1
decimal place before rounding, in case you have made an error
in your calculation.*

**4.** **B2 a)** Fully correct sketch **(B1 for any correctly labelled line.)**

**M1 b)** $PR^2 = 20^2 + 25^2$ or $PR^2 = 400 + 625$ or $PR^2 = 1025$
**M1** $PR = \sqrt{1025}$
**A1** PR = 32 miles or PR = 32.0 miles

5.	**B1** Rotation stated

   **B1** $90°$ clockwise or $\frac{1}{4}$ turn clockwise

   **B1** About $O$ or about $(0, 0)$

6.	**B3** Fully correct triangle drawn **(B1 for side _AB_ 3 cm long, allowing 2.9 to 3.1 cm. B1 for any angle correct, allowing ±2°)**

7.	**M1** Volume of cylinder $= \pi \times 12 \times 12 \times 30$
   **A1** Answer in range 13 564 to 13 574
   **M1** Area of base of cuboid $= 18 \times 16$ or 288
   **M1** $\pi \times 12 \times 12 \times 30 = 18 \times 16 \times$ height of metal
   or height of metal $= \dfrac{\pi \times 12 \times 12 \times 30}{18 \times 16}$
   **A1** Height of metal $= 47.1\ldots$ cm or 47 cm

8.	**M1** Angle $ABD = 128° \div 2$ or angle $ABD = 64°$ (Reason: angle at circumference is half the angle at centre)
   **M1** Angle $DBC = 180° - 64°$ or angle $DBC = 116°$ (Reason: angles on a straight line add up to $180°$)
   **M1** $x = \dfrac{180° - 116°}{2}$ or $x = \dfrac{64°}{2}$ (Reason: isosceles triangle)
   **A1** $x = 32°$
   **C1** All reasons given

> _Reasons must be clearly stated in order to be awarded the mark for quality of written communication. It can help to work out angles on the diagram._

9.	**C1** Smallest angle is angle $A$.
   **M1** $\cos A = \dfrac{b^2 + c^2 - a^2}{2bc}$ or $\cos A = \dfrac{7^2 + 6^2 - 5^2}{2 \times 7 \times 6}$
   or
   $5^2 = 7^2 + 6^2 - 2 \times 7 \times 6 \cos A$
   **A1** $\cos A = 0.714\ldots$
   **A1** $A = 44.4°$ or $A = 44°$

> _Remember that the smallest angle is opposite the shortest side. Make sure that you keep all the digits on your calculator display to avoid making rounding errors._

10.	**M1** Angle $A = 180° - 80° - 65°$ or Angle $A = 35°$
   **M1** $\dfrac{a}{\sin 35°} = \dfrac{8.4}{\sin 80°}$
   **M1** $a = \dfrac{8.4 \times \sin 35°}{\sin 80°}$
   **A1** 4.9 cm

11.	**M1 a)** $(2x + 3)(5x - 3)$
   **M1** $10x^2 + 9x - 9$
   **A1** $10x^2 + 9x - 9 = 27$
   **M1 b)** $(ax + b)(cx + d)$ where $ac = 10$ and $bd = \pm36$
   **A1** $(2x - 3)(5x + 12)$
   **B1** $x = 1.5$ and $x = -2.4$ **(Follow through from incorrect brackets)**
   **B1 c)** 6 cm

> _Remember that you can't have a negative answer for $x$ as it's a length._

12.	**B1** Two angles and a corresponding side

## Statistics and Probability (pages 104–105)

1.	**M1 a)** White : Blue : Red $= 2 : 3 : 1$
   **M1** Denominator of 6 used

   **A1** $\frac{1}{6}$

   **B1 b)** Valid reason given, e.g. $\frac{1}{6}$ of 10 isn't a whole number or must be a multiple of 6 counters in the bag

2.	**B1 a)** Circle around student at $(57, 2)$
   **B1** Doesn't follow the trend of the rest of the points
   **B1 b)** Line of best fit drawn starting at or before $(23, 1)$ to $(35, 1)$ and ending at or after $(58, 5)$ to $(62, 5)$

   **B1 c)** The more tests taken, the more hours of lessons (positive correlation).

3.	**a)**

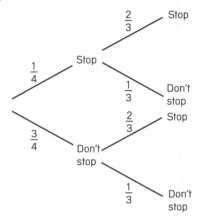

   **B1** First branches correct
   **B1** Second branches correct

   **M1 b)** $\frac{1}{4} \times \frac{2}{3}$

   **A1** $\frac{2}{12}$ or $\frac{1}{6}$

4.	**B2** Any two correct comparisons
   **B1** for each, e.g. on average it's hotter in town B (median 23°C in B compared with median 11°C in A); the range of the temperatures in A is bigger than in B (range for A is 40°C − 5°C = 35°C and range for B is 35°C − 10°C = 25°C); interquartile range for the temperatures in A is less than in B (interquartile range for A is 20°C − 7°C = 13°C and interquartile range for B is 30°C − 15°C = 15°C)

> _You'll be expected to compare the medians and a measure of spread. It's not enough to simply state facts without making a comparison._

5.	**a)**

   **B1** One bar to correct height or correct calculation shown
   **B1** Fully correct bars
   **C1** Axes labelled

> _For the quality of written communication mark to be awarded, all labels must be correct._

   **M1 b)** $\frac{40}{240}$ or $\frac{1}{6}$ seen

   **M1** $\frac{1}{6}$ of 500

   **A1** 83

# Maths Dictionary

**G 3-D coordinates** – coordinates that give the height, width and depth of an object; used to identify points in space using $x$, $y$ and $z$-axes.

**G Acceleration** – increase in speed or velocity.

**G Acute angle** – an angle that lies between 0° and 90°.

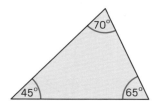

**G Adjacent side** – the side next to the angle or side being considered.

**N Algebraic expression** – a statement that uses letters as well as numbers.

**G Allied angles** – angles that add up to 180°.

**G Alternate angles** – angles formed when two or more lines are cut by a transversal. If the lines are parallel then alternate angles are equal.

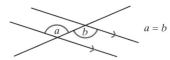

$a = b$

**G Alternate segment** – the 'other' segment. In a circle divided by a chord, the alternate segment lies on the other side of the chord.

**G Angle of depression** – the angle you have to turn downwards from looking along the horizontal to look at the ground or sea from the top of a tower, tree, cliff, etc.

**G Angle of elevation** – the angle you have to turn upwards from looking along the horizontal to look at the top of a tree, cliff, etc.

Angle of elevation

**G Angles at a point** – angles that meet at the same point and add up to 360°.

**G Angles on a straight line** – two or more angles, at the same point on a straight line, that add up to 180°.

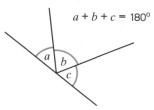

$a + b + c = 180°$

**N Approximation** – an answer that is nearly correct but not exact.

**G Arc** – a curve forming part of the circumference of a circle.

**G Area ratio** – the ratio of the areas of two similar shapes is equal to the ratio of the squares of their corresponding lengths.

**N S Ascending** – going up in order from smallest to largest.

**S Average** – a single number that represents or typifies a collection of values.

**G Average speed** – the total distance travelled divided by the total time.

$$\text{Average speed} = \frac{\text{total distance travelled}}{\text{total journey time}}$$

**N Balance** – keeping one side of an equation the same as the other side.

**S Bar chart** – a chart that uses bars of equal width to represent discrete data.

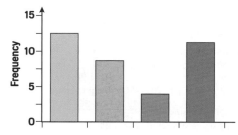

**G Bearing** – the direction measured clockwise from a North line at a fixed point. A bearing has three digits (for angles less than 100°, a zero, or zeros, is placed in front, e.g. 025°).

Bearing = 055°          Bearing = 130°

**S Bias** – a tendency either towards or away from some value; a question that invites a particular response, e.g. Do you agree that smoking is bad for you?

**N BIDMAS** – an acronym that helps you remember the order of operations: Brackets, Indices and roots, Division and Multiplication, Addition and Subtraction.

**G Bisector** – a line that divides a line, angle or area exactly in half.

**S Box plot** – a graphic representation of the distribution of a set of data, showing the median, quartiles and the extremes of the data set.

**N Cancel** – simplifying a fraction by dividing the numerator and denominator by a common factor.

**G Capacity** – the amount of space in a container or the amount of liquid it will hold.

**G Centre** – the middle point of something, e.g. the fixed point at the middle of a circle or a sphere.

**G Centre of enlargement** – the point from which the enlargement happens.

Centre of enlargement

**G Centre of rotation** – the point around which a shape can rotate.

**N Change the subject** – rearranging a formula to leave one variable on its own.

**G Chord** – a line joining two points on the circumference of a circle.

**G Circumference** – the distance all the way round the outline of a circle.

Circumference

Chord

**S Class** – the grouping of large amounts of data into different classes.

**S Class interval** – the width of a class or group, e.g. 0 g < mass of spider ≤ 10 g.

**N Coefficient** – a number or letter multiplying an algebraic term.

**G Collinear** – passing through, or lying on, the same straight line.

**N Common factor** – a factor that is shared by two or more numbers.

**N Common multiple** – a multiple that is shared by two or more numbers.

**N Complete the square** – writing a quadratic expression of the form $x^2 + bx + c$ in the form $(x + p)^2 + q$. This method can be used to solve quadratic equations.

**S Composite bar chart** – a bar chart that combines two or more groups of data into a single bar.

**N Compound interest** – interest that accrues from the initial deposit plus the interest added on at the end of each year.

**N Compound percentage** – a repeated percentage.

**S Conditional probability** – the probability that an event will occur given that another event has already occurred.

**G Cone** – a shape with a plane circular face, a curved surface and one vertex.

**G Congruent** – exactly alike in shape and size.

**G Construction** – an accurate drawing of a shape using a combination of ruler, protractor and a pair of compasses.

**N S Continuous data** – data that can take any value within a given range, e.g. length and time.

**G Conversion** – changing from one measure to another, e.g. metric to imperial.

**N G Coordinate** – a set of two or more numbers used to determine the position of a point, line, curve or plane in a space of a given dimension with respect to a system of lines or other fixed references.

**S Correlation** – the relationship between the numerical values of two variables, e.g. there is a positive correlation between the numbers of shorts sold as temperature increases; there is a negative correlation between the age and the value of cars.

**G Corresponding angles** – angles formed when a transversal cuts across two or more lines. When the lines are parallel corresponding angles are equal.

$a = b$

**G Cosine** – the cosine of an angle is the ratio of the length of the adjacent side to the length of the hypotenuse in a right-angled triangle.

**G Cosine rule** – a formula used to find the lengths of sides or the size of an angle in a triangle. The formula is given on the GCSE exam paper. $a^2 = b^2 + c^2 - 2bc \cos A$.

**G Cross-section** – the shape of a slice through a solid.

**N Cube number** – a number that is the product of three equal numbers, e.g. $4^3 = 64$

**N Cube root** – the cube root of a number is a number which, when cubed, gives the original number, e.g. $\sqrt[3]{64} = 4$

**N Cubic** – a cubic function of the form $y = ax^3 + bx^2 + cx + d$. Graphs of cubic functions are S-shaped.

**G Cuboid** – a 3-D shape with six rectangular faces.

**S Cumulative frequency** – the running total of frequencies calculated from a frequency table.

**G Curved surface area** – the area of the curved surface of a solid such as a cylinder or a cone.

**N G Cyclic** – a graph that repeats indefinitely in both directions.

**G Cyclic quadrilateral** – a quadrilateral with all four vertices on the circumference of a circle.

**G Cylinder** – a prism with a circular cross-section.

**S Data** – a collection of numbers or information.

**S Data collection sheet** – a sheet or log that is used to collect data.

**G Decagon** – a 10-sided polygon.

**N Decimal place** – the position of a digit after the decimal point.

**N Degree of accuracy** – the level of approximation that is made, e.g. to the nearest £, cm or thousand.

**N Denominator** – the bottom number of a fraction.

**N G Density** – the ratio of the mass of an object to its volume; the mass per unit volume.

**N S Descending** – going down in order from largest to smallest.

**G Diameter** – a straight line across a circle, from circumference to circumference and passing through the centre.

**N Difference of two squares** – the factorisation of $a^2 - b^2$ which equals $(a + b)(a - b)$.

**N Direct proportion** – two values or measurements may vary in direct proportion, i.e. if one increases, then so does the other.

**N Directed number** – a number that is given a '+' or '−' sign.

**N G Direction** – the line along which anything lies, faces or moves.

**N S Discrete data** – data that can only have certain values in a given range, e.g. number of goals scored, shoe sizes.

# Maths Dictionary

**ⓃⒼ Distance-time graph** – a graph that shows how distance varies with time.

**Ⓝ Elimination** – removing a variable from an equation.

**Ⓖ Enlargement** – a transformation of a plane figure or solid object that increases the size of the figure or object by a scale factor but leaves it the same shape.

Enlargement of figure by scale factor 2

**Ⓢ Equally likely** – the same chance (probability) of two events occurring.

**Ⓝ Equation** – a number sentence where one side is equal to the other.

**Ⓖ Equidistant** – a point the same distance from two or more other points.

**Ⓖ Equilateral** – a 2-D or 3-D shape with all sides of equal length.

**Ⓝ Equivalent fraction** – one fraction that has the same value as another fraction, e.g. $\frac{1}{2}$ and $\frac{2}{4}$ are equivalent fractions.

**Ⓝ Estimate** – an approximation of an actual value.

**Ⓝ Even number** – a number that when divided by 2 gives no remainder, e.g. 2, 10, 54.

**Ⓢ Event** – something that happens, e.g. tossing a coin.

**Ⓝ Exact** – an answer that is the true value.

**Ⓝ Expand (brackets)** – to expand brackets means to multiply them out to get an expression without brackets.

**Ⓢ Expectation** – the number of times you would expect an event to happen based on relative frequency (experimental probability) or theoretical probability.

**Ⓢ Experiment** – a test or a trial.

**Ⓝ Exponential** – containing, involving or expressed as a power (exponent); an exponential function is of the form $y = k^x$.

**Ⓝ Expression** – see **Algebraic expression**.

**Ⓖ Exterior angle** – an angle outside a polygon, formed when a side is extended.

Exterior angle

**Ⓖ Face** – the flat surface or side of a solid shape.

Face

**Ⓝ Factor** – a whole number that divides exactly into a given number.

**Ⓝ Factorisation** – finding one or more factors of a given number or algebraic expression.

**Ⓢ Fair** – an item or event that isn't biased.

**Ⓝ Formula** – an equation that enables you to convert or find a value using other known values, e.g. area = length × width.

**Ⓝ Fraction** – part of a whole. Fractions can be proper, improper or mixed.

**Ⓝ Fractional power** – a fractional power is a root, e.g. $16^{\frac{1}{2}} = \sqrt{16} = 4$ and $8^{\frac{1}{3}} = \sqrt[3]{8} = 2$

**Ⓢ Frequency** – the number of times that something happens.

**Ⓢ Frequency density** – $\dfrac{\text{frequency of class interval}}{\text{width of class interval}}$

**Ⓢ Frequency polygon** – joins the midpoints of data groups or classes in a continuous distribution.

**Ⓢ Frequency table** – an arrangement of data in a table.

**Ⓖ Front elevation** – the 2-D view of a 3-D shape or object as seen from the front.

**Ⓖ Frustum** – the remainder of a regular solid whose upper part has been cut off by a plane parallel to the base.

**Ⓝ Function** – a relationship between variables; one variable will depend on the other.

**Ⓖ Geometry** – the study of angles, triangles, circles and polygons.

**ⓃⒼ Gradient** – the measure of the steepness of a slope: $\dfrac{\text{vertical distance}}{\text{horizontal distance}}$

**Ⓢ Grouped data** – data that is organised into groups.

**Ⓖ Hemisphere** – half of a sphere.

**Ⓖ Hexagon** – a six-sided polygon.

**Ⓝ Highest common factor (HCF)** – the highest factor shared by two or more numbers.

**Ⓢ Histogram** – a chart that is used to show continuous data.

**ⒼHypotenuse** – the longest side of a right-angled triangle (always opposite the right angle).

**ⓈHypothesis** – a theory that is tested, by investigation, to see if it's true.

**ⓃIdentity** – an identity is similar to an equation, but is true for all values of the variable(s); the identity symbol is $\equiv$, e.g. $2(x + 3) \equiv 2x + 6$

**ⒼImage** – an object is transformed to give an image, e.g. after a reflection:

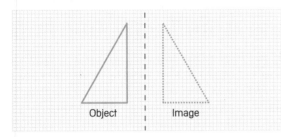

Object      Image

**ⒼImperial** (units) – units of weight and measurement, which have generally been replaced with metric units.

**ⓃImproper fraction** – a fraction in which the numerator is greater than the denominator, e.g. $\frac{9}{4}$

**ⓈIndependent events** – two events are independent if the outcome of one event isn't affected by the outcome of the other event, e.g. tossing a coin and throwing a dice.

**ⓃIndex** (also known as **power** or **exponent**) – the small digit to the top right of a number that tells us the number of times a number is multiplied by itself, e.g. $5^4$ is $5 \times 5 \times 5 \times 5$; the index is 4.

**ⓃIndirect (inverse) proportion** – two quantities vary in indirect proportion when, as one quantity increases, the other decreases.

**ⓃInequality** – a statement showing two quantities that aren't equal.

**ⓃInput** – the value put into a function.

**ⓃInteger** – any whole number, positive or negative, including zero.

**ⓃIntercept** – the point where a line or graph crosses an axis.

**ⒼInterior angle** – an angle inside a polygon between two adjacent sides.

**ⓈInterquartile range** – the difference between the lower quartile and the upper quartile, often found using a cumulative frequency graph.

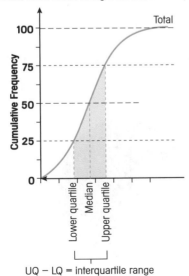

UQ – LQ = interquartile range

**ⓃIntersection** – the point at which two or more lines cross.

**ⒼIrregular** – shapes that aren't regular; sides and angles not equal.

**ⒼIsometric drawing** – a 3-D representation of an object in which the three axes are equally inclined and all lines are drawn to a given scale.

**ⒼIsosceles** – a triangle with two sides of equal length and two equal angles.

**ⒼⓈKey** – a guide on a statistical chart that tells you what each symbol means.

**ⓃLeast (lowest) common multiple (LCM)** – the lowest number that is a multiple of two or more numbers.

**ⓃLike terms** – terms in algebra that are the same, apart from their numerical coefficients, e.g. $2d$ and $8d$.

**ⓃⓈLimit** – a boundary, or the ultimate quantity or extent of something.

**ⓃLimits of accuracy** – the upper bound and lower bound are sometimes called the limits of accuracy.

**ⓈLine graph** – a graph where all the plotted points are joined by straight lines, e.g. a graph showing a hospital patient's temperature.

**ⓈLine of best fit** – a line (usually straight) drawn through the points of a scatter diagram, showing the trend and enabling you to estimate new values using original information.

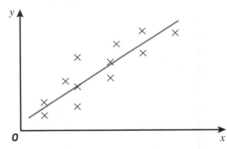

**ⒼLine symmetry** – the symmetry of a 2-D shape, giving two equal halves.

**ⓃLinear equation** – an equation that has no variable above the power 1, e.g. $y = 5x + 2$ is a linear equation.

**ⓃLinear graph** – a graph of a linear function, where all plotted points lie on a straight line.

**ⓃLinear inequality** – involves a linear expression in two variables by using any of the relational symbols such as $<$, $>$, $\leq$ or $\geq$.

**ⒼLocus (plural: loci)** – the locus of a point is the path taken by the point following a rule or rules.

**ⓃLower bound** – the bottom limit of a rounded number.

**ⓈLower quartile** – the reading that is $\frac{1}{4}$ of the way up a cumulative frequency graph or a data set.

**ⓃⒼMagnitude** – the size of something.

# Maths Dictionary

**Ⓖ Major sector** – the larger section of the circle between two radii and an arc.

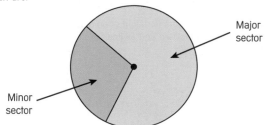

**Ⓖ Major segment** – the larger section of the circle between a chord and an arc.

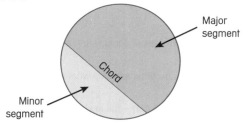

**Ⓢ Mean** – an average value found by dividing the sum of a set of values by the number of values.

**Ⓢ Median** – the middle item in an ordered sequence of items.

**Ⓖ Metric** (units) – units of weight and measure based on a number system in multiples of 10.

**Ⓖ Midpoint** – the point that divides a line into two equal parts.

**Ⓖ Minor sector** – the smaller section of the circle between two radii and an arc (see **Major sector**).

**Ⓖ Minor segment** – the smaller section of the circle between a chord and an arc (see **Major segment**).

**Ⓝ Mixed number** – a whole number together with a proper fraction.

**Ⓢ Modal class** – the largest class in a grouped frequency table.

**Ⓢ Mode** – the most frequently occurring value in a data set.

**Ⓝ Multiple** – if one number divides exactly into another number, the second is a multiple of the first.

**Ⓢ Multiple bar chart** – a bar chart that shows two or more groups of data side by side.

**Ⓝⓖ Multiplier** – the number by which another number is multiplied.

**Ⓝ Multiply out** – see **Expand**.

**Ⓢ Mutually exclusive events** – two or more events that can't happen at the same time, e.g. throwing a head and throwing a tail with the same toss of a coin are mutually exclusive events.

**ⓃⓖⓈ Negative number** – a number less than zero.

**Ⓝ Negative power** – the reciprocal of the same number to the positive power, e.g. $3^{-3} = \frac{1}{3^3} = \frac{1}{27}$

**Ⓖ Net** – a surface that can be folded into a solid.

**Ⓝ nth term** – the general term of a number sequence.

**Ⓝ Number line** – a line with a scale, showing numbers in order.

**Ⓝ Numerator** – the number above the line in a fraction.

**Ⓖ Object** – a shape.

**Ⓖ Obtuse angle** – an angle that lies between 90° and 180°.

**Ⓖ Octagon** – an eight-sided polygon.

**Ⓝ Odd number** – a number that when divided by 2 gives a remainder of 1, e.g. 1, 17, 83.

**Ⓖ Opposite side** – the side opposite the angle being worked on in a triangle.

**ⓃⓈ Order** – the arrangement into which items are put in ascending or descending sequence.

**Ⓖ Order of rotational symmetry** – the number of positions where a shape looks the same when it's rotated through 360°.

**Ⓢ Outcome** – the result of an event.

**Ⓝⓖ Parallel** – lines that stay the same distance apart and never meet.

**Ⓖ Parallelogram** – a quadrilateral with two pairs of equal sides. Opposite sides are parallel and equal in length and the diagonals bisect each other.

**Ⓖ Pentagon** – a five-sided polygon.

**Ⓝ Percentage** – the proportion or rate per 100 parts.

**Ⓝ Percentage change** – the change in the proportion or rate per 100 parts.

**Ⓖ Perimeter** – the perimeter of an enclosed area is the boundary or edge of that area; also the length of that boundary.

**Ⓝⓖ Perpendicular** – a line or plane that is at right angles to another line or plane.

**Ⓖ Perpendicular bisector** – a line that is drawn at right angles to the midpoint of a line.

**Ⓢ Pie chart** – a circular chart that can be used to illustrate statistical data.

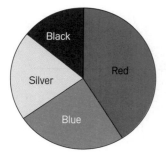

**G Plan view** – the 2-D view of a 3-D shape or object when looking down onto it.

Ground floor of a house

**G Polygon** – a plane (flat) shape with many sides.

**S Population** – the number of people who live in a certain place; any large group of items being investigated.

**N Position-to-term rule** – the rule that links the position of the term to the term, e.g. the position-to-term rule for odd numbers is 'double the position number and subtract 1'.

**NGS Positive number** – a number greater than zero.

**N Power** – see **Index**.

**S Primary data** – data collected by you for an investigation.

**N Prime factor** – is a factor that is also a prime number.

**N Prime number** – has only two factors, itself and 1.

**G Prism** – a 3-D shape that has a uniform cross-section.

Hexagonal prism

**S Probability** – the probability of an event occurring is the chance that it may happen, which can be expressed as a fraction, decimal or percentage.

$$\text{Probability} = \frac{\text{number of successful events}}{\text{total number of possible events}}$$

**N Product** – the result of two or more numbers being multiplied together.

**NG Proof** – an argument or explanation that establishes the truth of a proposition.

**N Proportion** – the relationship between things or parts of things with respect to comparative magnitude, quantity or degree.

**G Pyramid** – a solid shape with triangular faces meeting at a vertex.

**G Pythagoras' theorem** – the theorem which states that the square on the hypotenuse of a right-angled triangle is equal to the sum of the squares on the other two sides.

**N Quadratic equation / expression** – an equation or expression containing unknowns with maximum power 2, e.g. $y = 2x^2 - 4x + 3$. Quadratic equations can have 0, 1 or 2 solutions.

**N Quadratic formula** – a formula, given on the GCSE exam paper, used to solve quadratic equations:

$$x = \frac{-b \pm \sqrt{b^2 - 4ac}}{2a}$$

**N Quadratic graph** – the U-shaped graph of a quadratic equation.

**G Quadrilateral** – a four-sided polygon.

**NGS Quantity** – an amount.

**S Questionnaire** – a set of questions used to collect data.

**G Radius (plural: radii)** – the distance from the centre of a circle to its circumference.

**S Random** – something that happens by chance or without bias.

**S Random sampling** – a sampling method where each data object / person has an equal chance of being selected.

**S Range** – the spread of data; a single value equal to the difference between the greatest and the least values.

**N Ratio** – the ratio of A to B shows the relative amounts of two or more things and is written without units in its simplest form or in unitary form, e.g. $A : B$ is $5 : 3$ or $A : B$ is $1 : 0.6$

**N Rational number** – a number that can be written in the form $\frac{a}{b}$ where $a$ and $b$ are integers.

**N Rationalise** – to rationalise an irrational denominator is to make the denominator a rational number. To do this, the numerator and denominator are both multiplied by a surd (square root).

**N Reciprocal** – the reciprocal of any number is 1 divided by the number (the effect of finding the reciprocal of a fraction is to turn it upside down, e.g. the reciprocal of $\frac{2}{3}$ is $\frac{3}{2}$); a reciprocal function is of the form $y = \frac{k}{x}$ with $x \neq 0$

**N Recurring decimal** – a recurring decimal has digits that are in a repeating pattern like 0.3333 or 0.252 525. Recurring decimals are rational numbers.

**G Reflection** – a transformation of a shape to give a mirror image of the original.

**G Reflex angle** – an angle that lies between 180° and 360°.

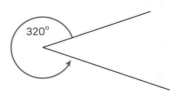

320°

**G Regular polygon** – a polygon that has sides of equal length and equal angles.

**S Relative frequency** – $\frac{\text{frequency of a particular outcome}}{\text{total number of trials}}$

**N Reverse percentage** – involves working backwards from the final amount to find the original amount.

**G Rhombus** – a quadrilateral with four equal sides but no right angles (a diamond). Opposite sides are parallel and opposite angles are equal.

# Maths Dictionary

Ⓖ **Rotation** – a geometrical transformation in which every point on a figure is turned through the same angle about a given point.

Ⓖ **Rotational symmetry** – a shape has rotational symmetry if, when rotated through 360°, there are a number of positions where the shape looks the same.

ⓃⒼ **Rounding** – replacing a number with a nearby number that is easier to work with or better reflects the precision of the data, e.g. 12 964 rounded to the nearest thousand is 13 000.

Ⓢ **Sample** – a section of a population or a group of observations.

Ⓢ **Sample space diagram** – a probability diagram that contains all possible outcomes of an experiment.

ⓃⒼ **Scale** – a marked measuring line.

Ⓖ **Scale drawing** – a diagram drawn to a given scale.

Ⓖ **Scale factor** – the ratio by which a length or other measurement is increased or decreased.

Ⓖ **Scalene** – a triangle that has no equal sides or angles.

Ⓢ **Scatter diagram** – a statistical graph that compares two variables by plotting one value against the other.

Ⓢ **Secondary data** – data used for investigation that has been collected by another person.

Ⓖ **Sector** – see **Major sector** and **Minor sector**.

Ⓖ **Segment** – see **Major segment** and **Minor segment**.

Ⓖ **Semicircle** – half of a circle.

Ⓝ **Sequence** (or **series**) – a collection of terms following a rule or pattern.

Ⓖ **Side elevation** – the 2-D view of a 3-D shape or object as seen from the side.

ⓃⒼ **Significant figure** – the number of digits in a number giving a required degree of accuracy.

Ⓖ **Similar** – the same shape but a different size.

Ⓝ **Simplify** – making something easier to understand, e.g. simplifying an algebraic expression by collecting like terms.

Ⓝ **Simultaneous equations** – two or more equations that are true at the same time; on a graph the intersection of two lines or curves.

Ⓖ **Sine** – the sine of an angle is the ratio of the length of the opposite side to the length of the hypotenuse in a right-angled triangle.

Ⓖ **Sine rule** – in any triangle the ratio of the length of a side to the sine of the opposite angle is constant, so $\frac{a}{\sin A} = \frac{b}{\sin B} = \frac{c}{\sin C}$. The formula is given on the GCSE exam paper.

ⓃⒼ **Speed** – how fast something moves.

Ⓖ **Sphere** – a 3-D ball shape in which all points of its surface are equidistant from its centre.

Ⓖ **Square** – a quadrilateral that has four equal sides and four right angles.

Ⓝ **Square** – to square a number is to multiply it by itself.

Ⓝ **Square number** – a number that is the product of two equal factors, e.g. $25 = 5^2$

Ⓝ **Square root** – the square root of a number is the number that, when squared, gives that number, e.g. $\sqrt{25} = 5$

Ⓝ **Standard index form (standard form)** – a shorthand way of writing very small or very large numbers; these are given in the form $a \times 10^n$, where $a$ is a number between 1 and 10.

Ⓢ **Statistics** – a collection of data used for analysis.

Ⓢ **Stem and leaf diagram** – a semi-graphical diagram used for displaying data by splitting the values.

Ⓢ **Stratified sampling** – a sampling method where the population is divided into categories and a sample is taken using the same proportion in each category as in the whole population.

Ⓝ **Substitution** – to exchange or replace, e.g. in a formula.

Ⓖ **Subtend** – an arc or line segment between two points is subtended by an angle.

Ⓝ **Surd** – a number written as a square root, e.g. $\sqrt{3}$. A surd is an exact number.

Ⓖ **Surface area** – the area of the surface of a 3-D shape, equal to the area of the net of that shape.

Ⓢ **Survey** – a collection of data for statistical analysis.

Ⓖ **Symmetry** – a 2-D figure can have rotational or line symmetry; a 3-D shape can have rotational or plane symmetry.

Ⓖ **Tangent** – a straight line that touches the circumference of a circle at one point only.

Ⓖ **Tangent** – the tangent of an angle is the ratio of the length of the opposite side to the length of the adjacent side in a right-angled triangle.

Ⓝ **Term** – in an expression, any of the quantities connected to each other by an addition or subtraction sign.

Ⓝ **Terminating decimal** – a decimal fraction with a finite number of digits, e.g. 0.75

Ⓝ **Term-to-term rule** – a rule that links one term to the next term, e.g. the term-to-term rule for even numbers is 'add 2'.

Ⓖ **Tessellation** – a pattern made by fitting together plane shapes (usually regular) without gaps.

Ⓢ **Theoretical probability** – a predicted probability; calculated using the fraction $\dfrac{\text{number of particular outcomes that can happen}}{\text{number of outcomes that are possible from the task}}$

Ⓖ **Three-figure bearing** – see **Bearing**.

Ⓖ **Transformation** – an action such as a translation, reflection, rotation or enlargement.

Ⓖ **Translation** – a transformation in which all points of a plane figure are moved by the same amount and in the same direction. The movement can be described by a vector.

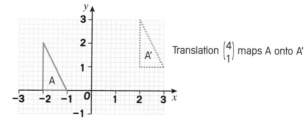

Translation $\binom{4}{1}$ maps A onto A'

Ⓖ **Trapezium** – a quadrilateral with just one pair of parallel sides.

Ⓢ **Tree diagram** – a way of illustrating probabilities in diagram form. It has branches to show each event.

**S** **Trial** – a test or an experiment.

**N** **Trial and improvement** – a method of solving an equation by making an educated guess and then refining it step-by-step to get a more accurate answer.

**G** **Triangle** – a three-sided polygon.

**G** **Triangular prism** – a prism with a triangular cross-section.

**G** **Trigonometry** – the branch of maths that shows how to explain and calculate the relationships between the sides and angles of triangles.

**S** **Two-way table** – a data-handling table to illustrate two variables.

|  |  | Team |  |  |
|---|---|---|---|---|
|  |  | Red | Blue | Green |
|  | 7 | 16 | 18 | 16 |
| Year | 8 | 15 | 17 | 16 |
|  | 9 | 15 | 15 | 15 |

**NG** **Unit** – means one, a single thing or number; the place-value position immediately to the left of the decimal point.

**N** **Unit fraction** – a fraction with the numerator 1, e.g. $\frac{1}{3}$, $\frac{1}{27}$

**N** **Upper bound** – the top limit of a rounded number.

**S** **Upper quartile** – the reading that is $\frac{3}{4}$ of the way up a cumulative frequency graph or a data set.

**NS** **Variable** – a quantity that can have many values, usually written as a letter, e.g. $x$, $a$, $k$.

**NG** **Vector** – a quantity with both magnitude and direction, e.g. velocity, force, displacement.

**G** **Velocity** – a more formal, and more correct, way of describing speed using both a magnitude and a direction, e.g. 30 mph towards the North.

**G** **Vertex** – in 2-D a point where two or more lines meet. In 3-D the corners of a shape, where the edges meet.

**S** **Vertical line graph** – a graph using vertical lines that can be used to represent discrete data.

**G** **Vertically opposite angles** – vertically opposite angles are formed when two straight lines intersect. The four angles add up to 360°.

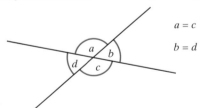

$a = c$

$b = d$

**G** **Volume** – the amount of space occupied by a substance or object or enclosed within a container.

**G** **Volume ratio** – the ratio of the volumes of two similar shapes is equal to the ratio of the cubes of their corresponding lengths.

# Formulae Sheet

**Volume of a prism** = area of cross-section × length

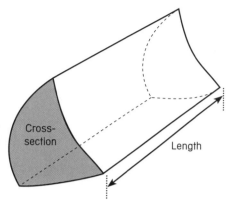

**Area of a trapezium** = $\frac{1}{2}(a + b)h$

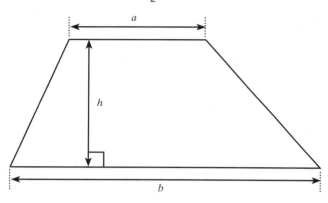

**Volume of a sphere** = $\frac{4}{3}\pi r^3$

**Surface area of a sphere** = $4\pi r^2$

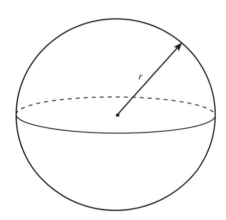

**Volume of a cone** = $\frac{1}{3}\pi r^2 h$

**Curved surface area of a cone** = $\pi r l$

**In any triangle $ABC$**

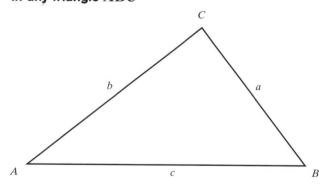

**The Quadratic Equation**

The solutions of $ax^2 + bx + c = 0$, where $a \neq 0$, are given by

$$x = \frac{-b \pm \sqrt{(b^2 - 4ac)}}{2a}$$

**Sine rule** $\dfrac{a}{\sin A} = \dfrac{b}{\sin B} = \dfrac{c}{\sin C}$

**Cosine rule** $a^2 = b^2 + c^2 - 2bc \cos A$

**Area of a triangle** = $\frac{1}{2}ab \sin C$